ONCE UPON A TIME-BEDTIME STORIES FOR ADULTS

RELAXING SLEEP STORIES FOR EVERY DAY GUIDED MEDITATION. A MINDFULNESS GUIDE FOR BEGINNERS TO SAY STOP ANXIETY AND FALL ASLEEP FAST WITH SELF HYPNOSIS.

BRAD RUSHFORD

© Copyright 2020 by Brad Rushford - All rights reserved.

The content contained within this book may not be reproduced, duplicated, or transmitted without direct written permission from the author or the publisher.

Under no circumstances will any blame or legal responsibility be held against the publisher, or author, for any damages, reparation, or monetary loss due to the information contained within this book. Either directly or indirectly. You are responsible for your own choices, actions, and results.

Legal Notice:

This book is copyright protected. This book is only for personal use. You cannot amend, distribute, sell, use, quote or paraphrase any part, or the content within this book, without the consent of the author or publisher.

Disclaimer Notice:

Please note the information contained within this document is for educational and entertainment purposes only. All effort has been executed to present accurate, up to date, and reliable, complete information. No warranties of any kind are declared or implied.

Readers acknowledge that the author is not engaging in the endearing of legal, financial, medical, or professional advice. The content within this book has been derived from various sources.

Please consult a licensed professional before attempting any techniques outlined in this book.

By reading this document, the reader agrees that under no circumstances is the author responsible for any losses, direct or indirect, which are incurred as a result of the use of the information contained within this document, including, but not limited to, — errors, omissions, or inaccuracies.

Introduction……………………………………………4

Chapter 1 The Plane……………………………………7

Chapter 2 A Fishy Tale………………………………..15

Chapter 3 The Dream Life……………………………24

Chapter 4 The Ocean's Song…………………………29

Chapter 5 The Changing Seasons……………………34

Chapter 6 Priorities……………………………………39

Chapter 7 Values………………………………………43

Chapter 8 Passion……………………………………..46

Chapter 9 Trip to an Exotic Resort………………...…50

Chapter 10 Harvesting Site For Fruits………………...59

Chapter 11 Dandelion Wish……………………..……69

Chapter 12 Autumn Dreams………………………......84

Chapter 13 The Eagle Takes You With Him………...…99

Chapter 14 Serenity…………………………………..104

Chapter 15 Courage………………………………..…107

Chapter 16 I Love Myself……………………………111

Chapter 17 Dancing With Dragon……………………...114

Chapter 18 12 Brothers……………………………..125

Chapter 19 The Robot 001…………………………..131

Chapter 20 The Mythical Land……………………...140

Chapter 21 The Old Woman In The Forest……………..147

Chapter 22 John Dietrich……………………………..151

Chapter 23 The Next Champion……………………...157

Chapter 24 The Young Saleh………………………...166

Conclusion…………………………………………..170

Introduction

First, let's talk about why do bedtime stories matter?

Well, do you remember going to bed as a child, hearing those wonderful stories your mom or dad, or even your guardian, tell you?

Those stories were a focal point of many children's lives. And, for most of us, remembering the fond memories that came with hearing those tales was something that helped many of us go to sleep within a reasonable time period, and have pleasant dreams.

Mindfulness, relaxation, and hypnotizing the body into a pleasant sleep is a key part of all this. The stories that you heard were whimsical tales, and while they might have seemed like much as a child, when looking back on this as an adult, it played a major role in our lives.

Bedtime stories were fun to hear. Sometimes, your parents would do voices. Other times, they'd just read the books quietly, and you'd pay attention each time. Sometimes they'd be tales you've heard plenty of times, other times they were tales they fabricated on a whim.

Regardless of what type of tales you heard, bedtime stories are wonderful for falling asleep. Most of them have soft, pleasant words that people love to hear.

Do you remember some of your former bedtime stories?

If you do, do you remember how they made you feel? The words you heard? The imagery you'd remember?

All of this plays a key role in why bedtime stories for adults are so important, and why, with each story you hear, you feel relaxed, at ease, and of course, able to sleep.

Each story will have fun, whimsical ideas, or imagery of different scenarios that you've been through before. The fun and excitement of going on a trip, the quests that you have, and even, a sleep fairy that will help you sleep. With every single story, you'll be spirited away on a wonderful adventure, one that's fun for you, and a good trip for everyone in the story.

If you have trouble falling asleep, just imagine yourself in the different scenarios each of these wonderful characters goes through. As you get spirited away in this adventure, you will notice that, with each time, and each place, it'll change for you. There are many different aspects to consider with each story, and many adventures to be had.

Also, don't think you'll hear the same story twice. While it might be the same words, there might be new adventures to be had, and new ideas that come forth.

Listening to bedtime stories will help foster your creative juices, help you improve you with ideas for the future, and also reduce stress. By listening to these ten wonderful stories, you'll be able to fall asleep soundly, and you'll be amazed at how refreshed you feel whenever you wake up.

Bedtime stories for adults also help with taking your attention off the troubles of life. If you're an adult, chances are you have some kind of stress. Whether it be work, bills, or even your family, that stress adds up, and it can make it hard for you to fall asleep. Many adults suffer from insomnia or can only sleep for a certain period of hours. That combined with the incredibly long work weeks, and also with the early morning shifts, it's not easy out there. But, with these bedtime stories, you'll relax your mind, you'll take your attention off the troubles you have, and promote relaxation, and of course sleep with each word you hear.

Many adults benefit from these types of stories. Some of us might wonder why, but if you take a moment to think about it, when was the last time you weren't focused on the stresses at hand, but instead on a relaxing, fun bedtime story that will help with sleep. If you can't remember, then you need these bedtime stories for adults.

With each story, each word uttered, each sound you hear, I hope they will lull you to sleep. It helps as well with shutting off your brain, helping you get focused on the different words you hear, and instead of feeling stressed and depressed, you'll get your mind off the troubles you have, and instead, feel brighter than ever.

With each of these stories, as you hear them when you sleep, you'll notice when you wake up you feel refreshed. That's because, with each sound, you'll hear words as well that are relaxing, soothing, and will help with sleep. Instead of stories that will keep you on your feet and alert, these small, short stories are simple, and yet very effective. If you have trouble relaxing, turning your mind off, and lulling the body to sleep, then this is for you. With each passing story, you'll feel your attention slowly slip away. Each sound you hear pulling you into a far-off land, into a realm of sleep that makes you feel happy, and at ease.

So, sit back, get comfortable, and listen to these relaxing bedtime stories. And with every one of these, you'll feel yourself whisked away into the tales they tell, and hopefully, you'll have pleasant dreams and a wonderful sleep as you continue to hear each story, and the creative, relaxing, and inspiring tales each one of them has to offer.

Chapter 1 The Plane

Today is the day of your vacation. For the longest time, you've been counting the days to your vacation, ready to see what the sights and smells of the community around you have to offer. You're so excited, but you managed to get some sleep as you drive to the airport.

The airport is a place that is usually filled with hustle and bustle, but this particular day, the traffic is not so bad. You drive to the airport. Your luggage is evenly placed in the car, and it looks quite nice stacked around. You know that it's going to be a fun vacation, but first, you have to make it to your destination in one piece.

The GPS is your guide, with it taking you to the parking lot of the airport. You park your car, then get out of the car, rolling your luggage alongside you. The shuttle pulls up, and you walk inside, but not before receiving some help with your luggage.

You sit down in the shuttle, breathing a sigh of relief. Your journey has begun, and yet you want to take a nice nap. Instead, you look out the window at the sights as the shuttle moves around. Soon, the shuttle pulls up right in front of the right airline. You step out, get your luggage, and roll it into the departure room.

As you stand in line to check in your bags and get your tickets, you weigh your bags beforehand. The weight is perfectly under the weight limit, and you smile knowing that you don't have to pay any extra fees to check in your bags.

The line moves a bit slowly, so you whip out your phone to see what is going on with the world. Then, you quickly sheathe your phone, seeing that the world is as messed up as it always is. You put away your phone, putting away your troubles for now. This week, you're going to take some time for you and you alone.

You soon arrive at the front counter and show your identification. Afterward, you receive your plane tickets, and the person behind the counter checks in your luggage. You watch the luggage roll down the conveyer belt until it's swallowed into the void. You hope your luggage has traveled as safe as yours. Then, you make your way to the security check.

Security check has another long line, so you stand in there, looking at the clock. You still have plenty of time for your flight. You know that you should always arrive early, and you're not stressing one bit. The line moves, and eventually, you put your belongings on the scanner's conveyer belt and step through the metal detector. Your security check was as stress free as any other security check could be. You have no pat-downs or any of that nonsense. You get your belongings, and then enter the departing section of the airport.

Here, there is a little mall filled with food and stores. Your stomach growls a bit. You were so excited for your trip, that you didn't even think about getting food. However, you realize that you should probably wait a bit. Instead, you should see where your gate is. You look at your ticket. Gate 33. You walk down the corridors, seeing everyone else waiting for their flight. Everyone looks as excited as you do, or tired at least.

Soon, you find your gate. It's not too far from everything, and you still have plenty of time to kill. So, you wonder what is going on at the strip mall.

You walk into one of the convenience stores. It has all sorts of souvenirs from the town the airport is in. They are cute, but a bit tacky and not what you're looking for. Plus, being airport merchandise, they are a little bit overpriced. You see some high-grade whiskey for sale. That may be a nice nightcap for the flight, but the price turns you off. You want to burn your money at the vacation spot, not beforehand. So, you ignore it, but still look around. The hottest bestselling books await you. However, not much catches your eye. As you leave the store, your stomach growls a bit. You want some nice food, but you're not sure where.

The airport holds many restaurants. Some of them fast food, others more of a dine-in experience. When it comes to food, you are not picky, so you see what foods they have.

You can get a nice chicken sandwich or sit down at a fish fry place. Or there is a little pub if you want some good food and drink before the flight. Despite it being an airport, none of the food is priced too heavily, so you decide to pick one. Whichever restaurant you're thinking of, you sit down and enjoy their food. Maybe you get yourself a tall glass of wine, or perhaps you have a nice breakfast for lunch. Regardless of your choice, you picked well, and you rub your stomach in fullness. Since it's going to be a long flight, and since airline food is hit or miss, it's wise for you to load up before you go to the flight.

You look at your clock. Still have plenty of time. So far, there are no delays, or anything to stress you out. You smile a bit, and then see what the rest of the airport has to offer.

There's a robot that rolls around the airport, with hearts for eyes. It's one of those guide robots that you can touch, and it can tell you where to go. It's quite friendly; well, it was programmed that way. You take a selfie with it, and then it rolls around on its merry way. You notice that it's low on batteries. It's probably going to go back to its charging station and take a nice, long nap. That sounds quite nice by now, does it not? However, you don't want to miss your flight, so you head back to the gate.

There's a decent half hour until boarding begins. So, you sit down, and you plug up all your devices on the seat's built-in USB slots. You imagine your phone and laptop getting its fill of energy as it takes a nap. This makes you want to yawn. It's going to be a long flight, so you should get yourself as comfortable as possible.

As you wait, you think about how much you've earned this trip. The past few months have been a little rough, and yet you've done enough to manage to pull this trip together. You should be proud of yourself, and you do have a bit of pride in the notion.

Your thoughts soon become daydreamy. You think about what you're going to do when you get there, where you want to go, and all that other good stuff. In fact, you start marking down your to-do list. Now that you've made a to-do list, you can rest a bit easier. This makes you smile a bit. You almost nod off, but then the boarding begins. You stand up and get in line. Then, you flash your plane ticket. As it's your turn to board, you show them your ticket. Ding. Now, you're walking down the tunnel to the plane. As you do so, you hear the hum of the plane's engine. It's such as nice. In fact, on your phone, you have a 10 hours audio file of nothing but plane engine noises.

As you walk inside the plane, you find your assigned seat. Luckily, it's right by the window, and the seat itself has everything you need. It reclines back, has removable handles, and is quite soft as well. Many planes are uncomfortable, but this is a rarity. You are happy to have chosen this flight, and you buckle yourself in. You spend but a moment securing the seatbelt, knowing if it's too tight, it won't be comfortable. Instead, you opt to keep it a little loose, but not so loose you can't wear it. Click-click, the buckle is put on and pulled. After that, you sit back, lightly pressing against the chair. You yawn for a moment, feeling all the fresh air hit your lungs. You do feel tired, but not ready to sleep just yet. You'll take nap once you're in the sky.

For now, you listen to the same welcoming speech, along with the general safety rules. Use the mask if an emergency happens. However, you know that a plane is one of the safest ways to travel, so you have no worries about it. Instead, you kick back the seat. The plane begins moving around, and then you hear that everything is safe to take off. The plane builds up its momentum, and then you feel the plane take off, soaring smoothly off the ground. You look out the window. Everything grows smaller as you go higher. It's quite a beautiful sight to behold. You see all the buildings and landmarks from high above, and it makes you feel special. Oh, how fun this trip will be.

As the flight goes higher and higher, things soon stabilize. You can now take off your seatbelt and get comfortable. It's expected to be a smooth flight with little to no turbulence. The flight attendant comes by and asks what you want. You ask for some wine and a cheese tray, or another snack of your choosing. You get a free snack with this flight, so you might as well take advantage of that.

After a bit, the flight attendant comes back with your stuff. You open the tray and begin eating the cheese. It's quite creamy and rich, and the wine is sharp and fruity. As you eat all these foods, you yawn a bit. The wine was the perfect little nightcap, or mid-afternoon cap, for you. You lie back, but not before making yourself comfortable.

See, this isn't your first time traveling, so you know how this works. You have a blanket, a fluffy neck pillow, and some sleep headphones. You put on the blanket and pillow first. You create a miniature fort for yourself as the plane cruises along the sky, your own little private abode that won't be disturbed until you land. Comforting. Relaxing. Already, you feel quite comfortable. Then, you put on the headphones.

The sound of the plane itself is quite ambient, and it's enough to make you fall asleep, but it's a flight, with the rhythm of the plane's white noise interrupted by coughing, babies crying, or by other noises people make.

As you turn on the white noise of the plane, you're now transported into another world. In this world, you have a private jet for yourself. You're kicking back and enjoying the flight, with no one around you. You feel comfortable thinking about this idea, and you wish this moment would never, ever end.

Your eyes grow heavier and heavier, and they soon close. Your mind does wander a bit and thinks about all the stuff you're going to do when you get there. From relaxing on the beach to getting lost in nature, this place that you're planning to visit has it all, and so much more. It was the perfect vacation spot, and not too much, either.

Soon, you fall asleep. You dream about what you're going to do for the vacation, and it feels like you've already arrived. These dreams last a good while, and when you wake up, you feel refreshed and ready to take on your vacation.

You look at your phone. The time matches the arrival time, adjusting for time zones, of course. You managed to sleep most of the way through your flight. Few people are as lucky as you are, so you let out a triumphant yawn and remove your headphones.

You hear an announcement. Soon, the plane will be landing. They thank you for choosing the airlines, and you buckle in your seat belt. You feel the plane going down, down, down, and you look outside to see all the sights. This place looks as beautiful as you imagined it, and you want to celebrate. The land grows closer and closer, until you feel the plane's wheels land on the runway. It's a bit shaky, but the landing is as smooth as possible. The plane eventually finds a gate, and as it does, you watch everyone pack their bags and leave. Rather than stand up, you savor this moment a bit. No rush. Soon, the plane clears out, and you grab your carryon bag.

As you leave the plane, you're greeted to the airport. The airport has plenty of signs greeting you, and as you leave the arrival gate, you see families celebrating as their loved ones come home. Although you have no loved ones, you do feel happy for them knowing that everyone has reunited.

You go down an escalator. Now, it's time for you to pick up your baggage. You believe that the baggage has made it safe and sound. You go to the baggage claim that matches your flight.

Everyone waits for their baggage, along with you. The conveyor belts soon come to life. Colorful baggage comes out of the gates of darkness. None of it looks like yours, however, but it is very relaxing to watch. You could almost fall asleep. You watch people claim their baggage, and then the next wave of baggage comes. Finally, you see your bag. This bag made it out perfectly unharmed. Ah, it feels so nice knowing that all your belongings are here and accounted for. You take your suitcase, and then look at the shuttle information. There is a shuttle that takes you to the train that takes you to your hotel, where you will settle in and begin this journey.

You find the nearest shuttle. It's just on time, and you get on it with no qualms whatsoever. As you do so, you relax and see the sights as the shuttle carries on. Everything looks so pristine, like a place of paradise.

Soon, you hop off the shuttle and go to the train station. You buy your tickets, and then the process happens all over again. It's still daylight, so it should be an easy journey. You soon hear the train approaching, and you get on.

The train goes faster than a bullet, and you get yourself situated. This time, you look at the sights again. Everything is so peaceful, so tranquil. You nod off. You got some sleep on the flight, but you know you want to pump your body with as much rest as possible. You soon wake up just as the train has arrived. You step out and grab your belongings.

After taking a cab to the hotel, you have arrived. It's a beautiful resort hotel, giving you all you need and more.

Checking in is surprisingly easy, and the bellhop takes all your belongings to your room. You follow them, and soon you're in your room. It's a beautiful suite just for you. You smile, knowing you've finally made it to your vacation spot. Soon, your vacation will begin, and it's going to be amazing. You lie on the bed, the fluffiness surprising you. It's been a long day, and you soon find yourself drifting to sleep. Tomorrow begins the best day of your life, and you want to prepare your body with some nice, restful sleep. It's going to be so lovely, it will.

Chapter 2 A Fishy Tale

Lure, check. Line, check. Pole, check. Everything seemed good for Paul's trip. The last little excursion of the summer, Paul wanted to catch the "big one" at Dreamer's Lake. While the size and description of the "big one" varied, people said that it was the biggest fish at Dreamer's Lake. Or maybe it was all a tourist trap. Either way, as soon as he was about to head out, he heard a gentle knocking at the door.

Paul opened the door of his quaint home to see Ryan at the door. Ryan was all dressed to fish, with a tackle box the size of a casket around his arms.

"All the other friends couldn't make it," Ryan said. "Work."

Paul let out a sigh. It was a battle getting the day off for him, but he thought that maybe Peter, Landon, and all his other friends could as well. Just one more trip with the boys was all he asked, but he assumed he'd settle for Ryan.

"Dang it," Paul said as he packed the rest of his belongings. The two hopped into Paul's truck, and with the gentle puttering of the truck leading the way, they were off.

Paul and Ryan did not say much during the journey to Dreamer's Lake. Occasionally, they'd look at each other, but besides that, they had nothing else to add to the conversation. Paul stared at the country roads in front of him.

The roads had that hypnotizing effect. Small twists and turns gave a bit of a mix-up, but otherwise, it was fields of corn and the occasional group of cows, munching on their hay and staring at the truck passing by. Someone's dog tried chasing after the truck, only to give up halfway.

Ryan looked out of the truck as well, at all the little country homes in front of him that were all lined up. Some were trailers, others were fancy houses. The scenery made Ryan yawn a bit.

"Tired?" Paul said.

"Yeah. Didn't get too much sleep last night. Was excited, you know? It's been so long since I fished." Ryan said.

Paul smiled. "It's going to be a good hour or two. You're free to take a nap if you wish."

Ryan laid his head down against the seat, and soon his eyes closed. Paul looked at Ryan, who already seemed to be in deep sleep somehow. Ah, if only the self-driving cars could come out. Both could get some extra Zs while the car gently takes them to their destination. But that technology seemed to be a few minutes away.

The truck continued to drift down the road, with not too much traffic blocking the way. Occasionally, he'd run into the Amish, but passing them was easy. As he passed the buggy, the trot-trotting of the horse filled his ears. He had to envy them a bit. Such a simple life they had. But he couldn't imagine the trip taking hours and hours on a horse-drawn buggy.

Ryan let out a snore, and Paul had to chuckle. Ryan was always the snorer of the bunch. Every time the crew spent the night, one of them wanted to put a giant cork in his mouth just to quiet him. It was like that sometimes.

About 30 minutes later, Ryan woke up, right after they hit a tiny bump. Surprisingly, he was quite energetic.

"So, what will you do if you catch the big one?" Ryan said. "Dreamer's Lake has a $1,000 reward. We could split it."

Paul chuckled. "As I keep saying, I don't think it exists. That reward has been around since we were children. It's just a little gimmick to get people to fish there. But I like Dreamer's Lake, as it is a decent fishing spot."

"Fair," Ryan said. "You're probably right. But in this boring life, you have to believe in something magical, even if it's a giant fish."

Paul had to chuckle at Ryan's remark, but he understood. Ryan had been through a lot in his life. He was sort of the black sheep of the group, coming from parents who always fought and put the blame on Ryan. Ryan grew up decently enough in spite of everything, but Paul could tell that Ryan had a deep sadness that he hid from everyone. It didn't help that, like everyone else, he had a mundane life and not much else going for him.

Perhaps a big fish could cheer him up. Even though it was supposed to be the thing of legends, he assumed that maybe there was a kernel of truth to it. Maybe there was a big fish, but it wasn't as big as people claimed.

After some time, Dreamer's Lake was right ahead. Sure enough, it was a bit packed. Cars lined up like little boxes across the parking lot. There was the parking lot, then a little park, and then the lake itself. He hoped that most people were there for everything else, not to fish.

Paul found a parking spot and stepped out, and they all double checked their gear to see if everything was in order. Everything seemed good to go for their fishing trip, and soon, they walked across the park. It was a nice day. That summer heat was still trying to cling on, but a cool breeze counteracted it. Couples lied down in the grass, staring at the nice clouds that drifted across the sky. Children played. In the wooded area, a photographer snapped a picture of a bird. Click. Click.

Paul had the temptation to join them, but with the sun setting earlier and earlier, he knew he had to act fast. Soon, they arrived at the boat rental place. They went inside, and the boat lady was behind the counter, her raspy voice moving through the area.

"What do you need?" she asked.

"Just a boat, please. Preferably a nice motorboat."

"Sorry, we're sold out of those."

"What about your lower ends?"

"Out of those, too."

"Then, what do you have?"

The swan boat's head bobbed back and forth as Paul and Ryan paddled across the river. Their movements stayed in a consistent rhythm, but even then, the boat moved quite slow. The swan glided across Dreamer's Lake in an almost trance-like movement, and it made both parties yawn quite a bit. This swan boat was meant for a relaxing trip, not one that was set on catching the biggest fish in the lake. Hopefully, the swan could do a whole lot more than gracefully glide across the water.

The real challenge was finding a spot to fish. Unfortunately, the lake was packed with fishermen and fisherwomen, and the two did not want any lines crossing, or any awkward stares as they fished. By the time they found a fishing spot, their feet exhausted themselves. The spot they found was right by a shoreline, located in a tiny corner around the lake. It was a little small, the chances are, they wouldn't find the big one here, but at least they could fish in peace.

They took out their fishing gear and began adjusting everything. They spooled the fishing line in a relaxing movement, and they made sure to hook their bait tightly around the hook. Then, there was a whoosh as they casted it into the water. The bobbers floated in the water, swaying back and forth as the ripples spread across the water.

The sun shined on these two fishermen as they waited for a bite. Until then, the two made some small talk. Talk that was small, yet had some meaning to it.

"How's the wife?" Ryan asked.

"She's doing good. I would have invited her, but fishing isn't her thing, you know."

"Ah. I'm talking to someone. Maybe it'll work out. She's a nice lady, but she still lives with her family and they treat her like a child. She wants to move in with me, but she doesn't have the money, and neither do I."

"That's silly. Watch out for those types. I'm sure she's nice, but you know."

The two exchanged some words back and forth, and then Paul's bobber went down. As it did so, Paul moved back a little, then started to reel it in. The fish did have a bit of fight in it, but it as it danced around underwater, its movements eventually stopped. Paul reeled it in. It was a nice catfish, the fish flopping a bit as the water dripped from its smooth skin.

"Well, at least we'll be eating well tonight," Paul said as he put the catfish in the bucket. It swam around, and the two resumed their fishing.

They kept fishing, and managed to catch a few more fish. Trout, blue gill, and a few other fish they didn't recognize went into the bucket. Many of

Dreamer's Lake's fish weren't native, but imported from all around the world. This gave a bit of credence to the idea that the big one was a big lie.

Soon, they had a bucketful of fish, and the cracks of the evening began to show in the sky. Soon, it would be time for everyone to go back. Once dusk hit, you'd get a good yelling at if you were still at the park. The last thing he wanted was to be treated like a teenage punk just because he was a little late.

Paul reeled in his line and sheathed his pole. "I think it's about time to get going," Paul said.

Ryan sighed. "Really? Just one more fish."

"All right," Paul said. "I'll watch."

The bob stood still in the water as the sun started to set. It was quite a beautiful sight to behold. In a way, it symbolized the end of summer and the beginning of a new season.

"I think it's about time to head out," Paul said.

"I guess so," Ryan said, and then he started to reel it back in. Suddenly, the bob dropped in the water like a cartoon character who discovered that gravity is a thing. The line began moving at a surprising pace, and Paul could tell that Ryan was using all his strength to keep the pole from flying out of his hands.

"It's a big one!" Ryan declared.

"No way," Paul said.

He looked down in the water. He could not see an outline of this fish, so he assumed it had to be deep down there. Knowing their luck, Ryan probably caught it on a log or something. However, Paul jumped in, grabbing the pole with his hands. He gasped at how heavy it was. Indeed, Ryan was holding on with all his might, and it made Paul gasp a bit.

The boat moved slightly, the swan boat going back and forth as they struggled. That thing was unstable enough already, but he made both parties gasp at the notion that the boat would probably be flipped over. Good thing they brought their life jackets, but this was the last thing they wanted.

Whatever was on the line wouldn't let go, and seemed to grow stronger as they resisted. It wouldn't be long before the line either broke, the pole flew into the water, or the boat fell over. They didn't see any other options.

However, Paul and Ryan still held on, and they looked at each other, with grins on their faces.

"Let's get this baby," Paul said, and they yanked the pole together. The fish resisted, and the boat tipped forward, almost spilling. But Ryan and Paul went back a little, balancing it out. Water flew into the boat, swishing as it did so. The boat continued to move closer to the dock, so at least they wouldn't have to go far should they have to spill.

The struggle seemed to go on forever, with both of them assuming that it would be the end. However, there was something that surprised them. The movements seemed to slow down just a bit. There was still a struggle, but it was a little less. The fish was getting worn out, and so were they, for that matter. Who would wave the white flag first? They weren't sure.

Soon, the movements stopped in the water, and both worked together to reel it in. Paul paddled while Ryan reeled it in. He struggled to do so, but eventually, there was an outline in the water. It had to be as big as the boat, if not bigger. How were they going to fit this thing into the boat?

They stopped at the dock. Paul managed to dock the swan boat, while Ryan climbed out, still holding on to his pole. With a mighty yank, with both their hands on the pole, the pole flew backward, and with it, a massive fish fell onto the dock.

Paul gasped. It didn't look like any fish he saw in any book. It had a silver color, with skin as smooth as a catfish, but some scales on its many fins. It had onyx eyes that did not blink as it struggled a bit, the hook between its fat lips. What crowd was left began to gather around the two fishermen, who smiled as they looked at each other?

After a few, a man came to the dock. He was dressed in his ranger outfit, and even he gasped.

"That is a big one! Even I thought this was a legend the park made up, but jeez, it's real!"

After that, everything was a bit of a blur. They returned their boat, and then to the information building, with the rangers saying they'd handle the big fish. As they went there, the lady behind the booth handed them a check.

"Don't spend it in one place," she said.

Ryan and Paul looked at each other, smiling, as they went outside. The park ranger was there.

"We've decided to take this fish into captivity for a bit to study it. Unfortunately, you can't take it home."

"I figured," Paul said. "Besides, we wouldn't even know what to do with it, anyway."

After a bit of talking, and the ranger repeating that he was so shocked that the fish existed, Paul and Ryan soon went to their car. As they did so, Ryan asked, "How are we going to spend the money?"

Paul looked at Ryan, and then handed him the check.

"Here you go. It's all yours."

"Huh?" Ryan said this with a gasp.

"You said you needed it for your girl. Plus, I just had a great time. It's been forever since I had a good night out with any friend."

"Thanks, but you can have it."

"No, you."

As they headed home, they argued about who was going to take the money. As they left, the sun began to set across Dreamer's Lake, the catch of the day swimming around in its new fish tank.

Meanwhile, Ryan woke up from his slumber in the truck. That night, Ryan dreamt of the fish, and the encounter he had with the tiny creature.

Chapter 3 The Dream Life

Just when you think life cannot get any worse than it currently is, either something magical can happen that will change your luck or it gets a little bit worse. Those are the only two options, after today you wonder how your luck will go, will it better? Or will your life come crashing down around you? You hear a knock on the door, your tired body drags you to answer it. You open the door to see a business woman, smiling largely as she hands you a heavy briefcase. Puzzled you don't want her to release the case. Who is this woman? Why is she here? Your brain struggles to process this, then she starts talking.

"You are the winner of the dream life sweepstake. You are the luckiest person on Earth right now, and everything is going to change for the better." This feels like a gimmick, surely, she will say you only need to invest, blah, blah, blah. So, you tell her that you are not interested and you just want her to leave you in peace so you can rest. She is dumbfounded as you shut the door in her face.

As you walk back to your bed, your phone rings. You answer it to hear a formal voice on the other line announce that he's a lawyer for the World's richest man, a man who died a few weeks ago. In his will he had a list of names, people that he had encountered in his life...everyone from the school librarian in primary school to a drive thru window cashier at the McDonald's. Anyone he met, he added them to this list. Upon his death he wanted his list to become a sweepstakes for his fortune, but his money ruined his life. It tore apart his family, it made him greedy, it made him lazy. He wants someone to be able to live out their dream life, through his will, but with guidance. The lady at the door is the first step towards guiding you to accepting this fortune. After the lawyer explains, you still can't seem to process this. You don't think you met this man, and if you had...would you be so lucky as to win his entire fortune?

Is this that point where your luck changes? Will it be the best thing that ever happened to you? Or will you waste your time? Isn't it worth the amount of time, just to listen to the lady? What harm can it do? You turn around and walk back to the door. Allowing the woman to enter your home. You have a seat at the table and she opens the brief case. "First, we will start with a questionnaire. I am to guide you to a dream life, not just hand you a fortune. Once that I am certain you are ready to have the fortune, it will be all yours." You hesitantly agree, still feeling this is too good to be true.

What is your dream job, do you wish to earn fulfillment through your work, or is it a means to an end? You decide you have nothing to hide from this woman, so you tell her the truth. She nods and moves on to the next question.

What is your dream family? Do you have it? Would money change your family, for the better or for the worse?

If you could live anywhere in the world, where would you live? Why would you live there?

"Ok, that takes care of the basics. Give me a few moments and I'll be back soon." As she leaves the room, you suddenly find yourself a bundle of nerves. Your body is tense and achy. You want to relax yourself, not let this work you up. So, you take a deep breath as you stretch and flex the muscles in your body. As you exhale slowly, you allow the muscles to relax. You can feel a warm tingling sensation rushing through as you repeat the process. You keep breathing slowly, becoming aware of your body. It is heavy and tired, you relax into the chair and focus on the simple task of breathing and allowing your body to rest. The lady enters the room again and you feel relaxed, maybe this is for the best. "Now, we will start building your dream life. Starting with some major purchases, then working through the minor ones so we can organize your new life. What type of car do you wish to have? Do you need anything custom on it?" She hands you a form, as you order your dream car.

You think about all the cars you've wanted throughout your life, until you finally settle on one. You try to keep in mind, this is because you're not spending your own money. This is just a 'dream' car for a reason. Think of every elaborate detail you would want in that car, including a personal driver, if that's what you want. Once you have etched every detail into that paper, hand it back to her.

"Now, we can decide on your land. I got some listings in the areas you described as your dream location. Please, look over these and see if any of them are what you had in mind."

As you look through the real estate listings, you see so many perfect opportunities. They are exactly where you would want to build a dream home. You look at the surrounding areas and you can picture the beautiful landscape now. Hearing the local noises. Smelling the scents, feeling the peace it would bring to you to be there now. You realize you've held onto this particular listing for a while. You let her know this is the one you like the most. Her fingers fly across her phone as she informs you that the land now belongs to you. All the paperwork will be signed at the end. You are dumbfounded as you look at her and ask, "Why me? How did I know this man, why would he want to give me this dream life?"

"I don't know the details. I just know that your name was on his list, and it is the name that was selected. My job is planned out in exquisite details, which is why we are able to shuffle along through these tasks. You are in fact a very lucky person, with a great fortune. Let's not lose momentum now, the sooner we have everything in order, the sooner you get to experience your dream life. The best contractor and his team are prepared to draw up your dream house when you are ready. They will be here shortly, I have just sent them the land, so they will have a better idea on how to make things work for you. While we wait for them, are you happy in your current dwellings? Or do you want a new temporary home while your dream home is being constructed?"

You think long and hard on the question. Now that money is apparently not a problem, what do you want to do while your dream home is being constructed? Do you want to live here and just wait? Do you want to hire movers and move into a nice upscale place? Or a place far away from everyone and everything while you process your new life? Surely, you'll want to escape the media, if you stay in your current dwellings, you need people to help keep the media off you. Or maybe you'll step into the spot light and shine, embracing your dream life. When you thought of what you wanted you let the lady know and she assures you that nothing will be a problem. All your wishes for your new life will be answered.

The contractor has arrived with his team, only now that it is not just this lady in front of you, or the voice on the phone from earlier, the reality is really sinking in. Your life is going to become everything you've ever wanted. As they bring in their things and get settled you start to wonder what you will do with your life? With all your worries fading quicker and quicker into your past, what does your soul want? When everything material in this world becomes easily bought, what are the things you need to work on? How can you be the person that you truly want to be? Do you need all this money to accomplish your goals? Will it make your life that much easier? Probably, but when all those little inconveniences are covered, and no longer troublesome, does your life feel empty or is there a vast opening that you can now explore? Will you travel the world? Will you fund new charities or help those already established?

The contractor introduces himself and starts to ask questions about your dream home so that they may begin the process...you feel your mind flooded with images of beautiful houses, but you don't know where to start. You inhale and exhale and decide right now to start becoming the new you, as you describe this home. This home reflects who you are as a person. Build it from the ground up. Describe how you want your base, in detail, build your dream home, until you drift into a deep peaceful rest. When you wake up tomorrow, you will be this new person with a strong base to work on your dream life.

Chapter 4 The Ocean's Song

You are on a small, remote island. The sand and ocean pristine, the vegetation is full and lively. Simple living is a way of life here and it feels like time itself passes slower. There is no hurrying about as you decide to go for a walk on the remarkable beach. The sun is low in the sky, the air is warm and perfect. The glistening sand is soft, almost white in color as your feet sink slowly and softly into the warm, welcoming sand with each step. Allowing the warmth to spread around your feet, but not stick as you gracefully stroll along the water's edge. The water to your right is a beautiful Caribbean blue, with white foam bubbles as the waves gently caress the beach.

As you slowly walk you can hear the ocean; seeming to swell in the great distance, but when it reaches you it is a soft whisper. A remnant of the great wave it once was. If the ocean were a person, what things could it tell you? Would it tell you of its survival? Of its suffering? Of the astounding life it provides for many? Would it sing it in a song? Listen to the ocean. Can you hear it sing? Is it a sweet lullaby? Is it singing ever so softly? As you watch the waves dancing to the song you yearn to feel them caress your skin. Walking just barely into the water, feel the waves crash upon your tired feet.

Feel the sand beneath you give way as the earth pulls you down. Stand still, allow the ocean to embrace you. The coolness of the water quickly passes as the next wave surrounds your ankles. Allowing your feet to sink just a little further into the warm sand. As the water sways out you feel your body call out to it to come back. It does, it always does. The water goes out, it comes back in. The ocean breathes, just like you. The water comes in, you take a deep breath, filling your lungs with oxygen. You breathe out, the water rushes out. Carrying that sweet oxygen from your head down to your emerged toes. Listen to the ocean's song as it breaths with you. Swaying with the gentle sounds, settling your body down into the earth. Like the roots of a tree, you are beneath the earth now while still reaching for the sky. Anchored into the life-giving solid base of this planet.

You hear a giggle in the distance, instantly recognizing the tinkling sound; as a young child plays on the beach. Such pure joy and happiness pull you towards it. As you approach the child you give a warm welcome. They giggle and continue in their own little world of happiness. Slightly ahead there is a bench. You decide to sit for a while and just enjoy the scenery. The sun low over the ocean, the palm trees behind you swaying with the light breeze. The sand soft and warm, glistening the reflection of the sun. You lie your head back allowing your neck to relax as you listen to the sounds. The ocean singing its song as it breathes in and out. The child's soft giggles of pure joy and happiness. This place is paradise, it is as if there is no room for the cloudy thoughts of tomorrow. For the doubts in the recesses of your mind. All your troubles need to escape.

You feel a soft tap on your shoulder and you open your eyes to see the sweet child smiling at you. The child hands you a container of bubbles. Without speaking any words, you know this child is asking you to blow the bubbles for them. You feel silly, playing with this child, but there is no harm. You open the bubbles, dip the wand, and exhale gently. A stream of iridescent bubbles spews forth. The child giggles and dances as they fall around them. You feel yourself smile, knowing the very simple effort you put forth caused someone else such great joy is a rewarding sensation. You repeat a few times, but the child's parent is calling for them. They run off abruptly, you try to call them back, hand them the bubbles, but they are gone.

Left alone with your thoughts and the child's play you speak to your inner child. What do you want in life? You ask it. As your mind responds, you blow a big, soft bubble and watch it drift off. Your mind is settled making the exchange, a bubble is just as good as an answer on this island. Anything that is on your mind, form it into the bubble. Blow it away. No matter how big or small, each bubble is satisfying to just let go. Collect each and every thought you have, pouring them into this bubbling liquid. Dip in the wand, and blow them all away. This is your time for relaxation. Nothing stands in your way except your mind. Who controls your mind? Control each thought as you form consistent beautiful bubbles. Watch them drift over the ocean. Carrying your troubles away from you.

Watching the bubbles disappear over the ocean you notice the sun is now even lower in the sky. There is still no rush. Nothing to hurry to, nothing to worry you; simply be and enjoy. The sun is wrapped in magical, striking colors. Above the sky is pink, turning to a warm orange and yellow glow surrounding the sun. The clouds white up high and sinking down to grey, to darkest of blue just above the ocean. The purple just above the horizon starts so soft near the sun and sinks down into the black of night. You can see the stars starting to wake up throughout the sky. Twinkling to life as the day shifts into the night.

With the darkness settling in you decide to make your way to your island retreat. The sand is different now. No longer warm as your feet sink into the calm coolness of the sand is still welcoming. One thing that is consistent is the song of the ocean. Although it is no longer a whisper, it sings louder, encouraging you to experience the steady cadence. Breathing in, breathing out as you meander your way to your home away from home. You can see the soft glow of the porch light, but you also see the shadow of the hammock in the side yard. The hammock calls to you, you aren't ready to turn off the ocean's song just yet.

Nestled between two great palm trees, you climb into the hammock. As you sway, you find your center of balance. Focusing your breathing with the faint song of the ocean. Breathing gently in, you allow your feet to rest. Breathing out you allow your legs to sink into the sturdy net beneath you. Breathing in, your back and stomach settle and as you breath out they sigh into the perfect position of comfort. Resting your arms comfortably you allow the breath to continue influencing your relaxation. The frogs and insects start to come alive and sing their own songs. They do not distract you; your song has become your own reflexive action. Breathing in and breathing out is the natural order. You no longer need to think of actively doing it, your body will just continue to do this as your muscles stay relaxed and your bones settled.

You peer up through the outline of the huge palm fronds and see every star in the night sky. The moon is a tiny sliver, as if handing over the spotlight of the night sky to the stars. Allowing them to share their beauty with you. You begin to draw patterns and shapes between the stars. Do you see the bear? The man with his bow and arrows? The queen sitting upon her throne? The swan, flying gracefully through the night? Tracing the connections between each group. Do you just see many lines, connecting all the stars? Focus harder, look at each individual star.

Imagine how much life and potential there is that is seeing this same star as you at this very moment. In the big scheme you are no different than any other, yet you are a thousand ways unique. You have so much inside you, but you are in control of it all. Every thought you have, is a part of you. You control where that thought is stored. If it's troublesome, blow it away in a bubble. If it is pleasant, explore it. This is your time, your vacation, you are everything in existence and you are nothing but quiet and stillness. Allow your eyes to rest like the rest of your body. Let them be sleepy and at peace. Give your mind control of your entire body; your mind gives you peace, joy, and rejuvenation. Nourish it, enjoy the song of your mind as you drift into oblivion.

Chapter 5 The Changing Seasons

The seasons, change. It is not sad, happy, or with frustration, it just simply is. Just like the seasons change, so do we. Do you let your seasons' simply change as you move through life, or do you try to force them to stay the same or force them to move on too soon? Just like the rotation of the Earth, there are some things in this life you cannot control. These are things we need to learn to accept as graciously as possible. It is not always easy, but with practice and knowledge, just like everything else in life; we learn to deal with our seasons changing. You can think of your season as a day in your life, or maybe a time period. However large scale or small scale you need to picture the answer is what feels right for you, which brings you the most peace.

Imagine you are a great big oak tree. As you stretch your body tall, your roots have grown deep down into the earth. The rains you have felt, have made you dig down deeper, sturdy your foundation. Your bark is tired as it keeps your body rigid. The early spring wind blows through, making you sway a little as you creak and sigh. Think of your bark as your blanket, pull it close to you, let it surround you in its warmth as it supports your growth. Let this growth warm you from the inside out. Focusing your breathing as it spreads from deep down on the tips of your roots, all the way up to new leaves blossoming to life. As you feel the sun warming you up from the outside, you are now completely surrounded in warmth. The sun is essential for your growth, feeding your joy and happiness. Your branches spreading out and settling into their new relaxing fullness as your thoughts in your busy mind appear as leaves upon your branches. Your leaves filling out with new green as all the thoughts fill every single leaf. This may be your early life, from the time you were a child, growing into a young adult. Each leaf holding new meaning, new thoughts, new memories, anything that rests within your mind can be found on a new green leaf. As you picture each thought in your mind, blossom it into a leaf. This can be any thoughts you have, maybe from your early, or maybe just from today. Once your tree is full of new green thought leaves, so full it cannot hold anymore, it is time for the day to change.

As the days begin to grow longer, the sun warmer. Let your thoughts begin to settle. As each thought becomes full, it grows into a deep summer green. Some thoughts are fleeting in your summer days, maybe you enrich the lives of the insects as they rest and sing you beautiful songs in return for some nourishment from your thoughts. It's ok to let go of these leaves, let the insects take them. Maybe a summer thunderstorm passes through. The rains and wind taking away your thought leaves before they're ready to go on their own. This is natural, summer is an enriching time in our lives, but it can also be unpredictable. During summer there is growth, mature growth. Grow from being a young adult, to an adult. Grow from being too busy to experience life to know there are things in life you should slow down to enjoy. Summer can be warm and pleasant, or it can be sweltering and nearly unbearable. You are a full, deep green oak tree. You are tired and your leaves rest heavy on you, the summer days are almost over and you can feel the air calling out for you to take a rest.

Maybe Summer ,for you, is going from a young adult to an adult. Maybe it was the rough part of the day that is time to just let go of. Just as the seasons will surely change, so will your life, so will your day.

The air becomes crisp, your senses sharpened with wisdom. You know the joy of growth has come and is nearly time for its end. You feel the deep green thoughts begin to change. What had once felt urgent and important fade to wonderful and colorful shades of yellow, orange, and red. The change being so visible, you know it is nearly time to let them go. As the smallest rustle or whisper of wind causes those thoughts that are too full to drift slowly to the ground. Let them go, they are no longer part of what you need. What your mind needs now is relaxation and wonderful peace. It is Autumn, it is Fall, it is time to let go. Watch in wonder as your thoughts become less meaningful, less impactful on your life as they drift slowly to the ground. Surrounding you in a colorful blanket.

Maybe Autumn for you is going from an adult to accepting the wisdom and maturity that come with age. To embracing that age with pride, knowing that it is just a season you must go through. Maybe it is acceptanceble for the things you cannot change, but embracing the wisdom that you get from experiencing the many trials and tribulations throughout life. Or is it just the part of the day where you can slow down, breath, and start to relax. Isn't it peaceful knowing that all the growth, and business of the day is finally over... you can let the responsibilities drift away like the leaves surrounding you.

You feel a change in the air around you, the coolness begins to become frigid. This is your mind reminding you of all the leaves you have lost. This is the harshness of Winter. This is the hardest season to control or predict and this is what you experience at the end of each cycle of seasons. Whether it is the end of your day, or towards the end of your life. Maybe you have a short winter and the frigid night passes quickly. Or maybe you are packed up tight and you're prepared for the harshness of winter. I am here to help you deal with your Winter. Remember that you are a strong oak tree, with a thick, warm blanket of bark to protect you. Your leaf thoughts have gone and left you bare to the dark and cold of the night. How do you get through this desolate loneliness? Just your body and your empty mind. For starters you are not alone. You are the greatest company that you will ever know. You know yourself better than anyone. You know what you want from life. Your mind knows how to get it, even if you're unsure, deep down you know you will figure it out. Stop thinking of Winter as the end of the cycle. It is your new beginning, a chance to start over. It is the peaceful calm where you know you must rest; before the life of Spring wakes up. During winter, you don't worry about what Spring will hold. Just allow the Winter to surround you, live in it.

Allow the snow to fall, surround you. It is not cold, but it is heavy. Let its weight be a comfort as it forces your muscles and your body to stay relaxed. If you feel tense, the heavier the blanket of snow will become, until you have finally given over to the relaxation. Allow your mind to welcome the white, peaceful new blanket surrounding it. Your day is over, there is no reason to think of it any longer. It is not yet time for Spring, so do not think of tomorrow. Let this be your day to enjoy Winter. Live in the state of rest.

Maybe Winter for you is the final stage of life. A time where you have no more worries. You are retired, your family is settled and happy. You have come to accept that life has been through most of its highs and it is time to just rest. Enjoy being in complete calm, nothing is expected, nothing is anticipated. Maybe Winter is the end of the day. The time at night when your mind has gracefully decided to let go of the day's thoughts. To let you drift off to sleep with no expectations. Just calm and blissful sleep to rejuvenate your mind, your daily Winter. This rest is needed, so that your mind can prepare itself for the busy Spring ahead. This is the season that we all try to skip over, because we feel it isn't vital for growth.

One can argue that it is the most vital, because without this period of rest; the more ragged we become. The harder our other seasons seem. As the seasons' change, so must we. We need to be able to set aside the time of our days to transition smoothly. When it is time to let go, let the season change. Embrace the end of the cycle, rest in your Winter before you move on.

Chapter 6 Priorities

Jack was a 65-year-old man who was rather proud of the life that he had built for his family. He had worked hard since his teenage years and done everything he could over the past five decades to give his family the life that he felt they deserved. He spent long hours working as a laborer, pulling in as many extra shifts as he could so that he could provide for his family. Thanks to his hard work, his wife was able to stay home and raise their three children in a beautiful home that he had purchased for them. He filled the home full of furniture, food, and various treasures based on whatever his family desired to have. When his family wanted to go on vacation, he would work overtime to afford the added expense and would always plan dreamy vacations that brought his family great joy. They would visit places like Disney Land, Martha's Vineyard, and even Arizona to see the desert. His family traveled to many different places enjoying all of the different views and creating many different memories.

Although he seemed to be around fairly frequently, Jack never felt as though he was able to truly relax and enjoy his time with his family. He had grown so used to working hard that he always had to be doing something: fixing something, building something, cleaning something, or moving something around. No matter what day it was or how much work he had already done, Jack would always do more work than what was reasonable because he simply felt uncomfortable just sitting around and enjoying the presence of his family. To Jack, nothing felt more satisfying than retiring after a hard day of working and feeling the comfort of his pillow rising to meet him.

One day, when he turned 66, Jack found that he was not feeling as good as he used to. For a while, he chalked it up to being older and dealing with regular pains of old age. After a few months, however, Jack could no longer deny that he was experiencing some fairly serious symptoms. His symptoms had grown so strong that he could no longer do the labor work that he once had, so he quit his job and retired to please his family. If it were up to him, Jack would have found a way to keep working despite his setbacks with his health. Still, he listened and retired, as he knew he probably should.

Shortly into his retirement, even simple things became challenging for Jack. He could no longer work like he used to, and eventually, even smaller tasks like climbing the stairs or going for a walk to the mailbox became more of a challenge for him. Finally, with his family's insistence, Jack went to visit a doctor to see why he might be experiencing such hardship with his health. It was from that appointment that Jack went on to learn that he was terminally ill with cancer and that he had waited too long to be checked so he was beyond the point of being able to be cured.

Jack and his family were shocked by this news as they realized that the once vital and virile man was quickly falling apart before their very eyes. Within weeks, Jack could no longer climb the stairs at all, and sometimes he even had troubles holding his coffee mug or pouring himself a glass of water. His wife, Susan, had to do everything for him. Being unable to do anything for himself made Jack angry and embarrassed, as he had always been a very proud and self-sufficient man. He spent the past five decades taking care of this woman; he did not feel as though he needed his wife to be taking care of him, now.

As time went on, Jack's anger turned into sadness. His family would all visit him in his home and bring their young children around, and everyone would play and get along like they always had. This time, though, Jack was forced to sit there and observe and partake in the conversation as he could no longer get up and find some work to do to keep himself busy. It was during these visits that Jack grew to understand just how much he had missed by being so deeply devoted to his work ethic and not spending enough time paying attention to his family. He realized that he had missed countless birthdays, holidays, anniversaries, and even just simple day-to-day memories because he was so absorbed in his need to work that he never truly sat down to enjoy his family until it was almost too late.

At first, Jack was angry with himself for not having spent more time with his family. He could not understand how foolish he had been by working so intensely and missing out on the majority of his children's and grandchildren's lives. Then, he became angry that he felt he had no choice but to work that hard to be able to give them the life that he wanted them all to enjoy. Eventually, Jack found himself thanking his own life for giving him enough time to see what he had missed and for giving him the opportunity to make up for it now before it was too late.

One day, when he was talking to his son, Jack decided to offer him some advice about his work ethic. Jack said, "Son, when I was your age my priorities were all wrong. I thought I had to work the hardest, be the best, and make the most money to make my family happy. Your mother told me she wanted me around more and wished I was there for the kids more, and I justified my actions by saying that I was there financially to support them. But that's not enough, son. In life, simply giving someone our money and hard work is not enough. If you truly want to be happy and live your best life, you take some time every single day to sit with those kids of yours and enjoy them. Never work so hard that you miss birthdays, anniversaries, or even just those special suppers each night. Be there for as many moments as you can, son, because believe me, one day they will have all slipped by. I realize now my priorities were wrong, and I taught you wrong. The true priority you need to have in life is to be able to provide for your family, but not just with finances. Prioritize the opportunity to provide them with your time, your attention, and your love. Believe me, son. It will make a world of difference."

Jack's son never forgot this story and went on to live by these words even long after Jack had passed. In fact, Jack's son went on to teach his own children about the value of these priorities, and they went on to teach their children! So, thanks to Jack and his hard work, his entire family was able to enjoy more quality time together for generations to come because he took the time to realize that prioritizing finances was not the only important thing in life. Time, attention, and love also mattered when it comes to providing for your family and truly taking care of them, and yourself.

Chapter 7 Values

Sarah was an average small-town girl, raised in a farming community in the southern states. For as long as Sarah could remember, she always dreamed about leaving the small community and heading out to the big city to enjoy a fast-paced lifestyle. Sarah would dream about hopping in her car when she was 18, heading off to college, and then starting a career in a big city like New York or Los Angeles. She would draw pictures of it and hang it on her wall, dream about it, and talk about it any chance she got. Her parents were sad that Sarah wanted to leave so badly, so they always did their best to show Sarah the value of living in a small community. They did this by teaching Sarah how to establish friendships with her neighbors, how to become self-sufficient, and how to market herself so that she could share their family business with their neighbors. Sarah's parents ran a produce store from their farm, so Sarah gained great business knowledge from her years spent working on the farm.

Despite how hard her parents tried to keep her from leaving when she turned 18, Sarah simply could not wait to leave for college and then start her city life. Just as she always planned, she packed up her belongings in her car and left for college. Sarah spent four years getting her business degree so that she could move to New York and work for corporate America. Although her parents did not fully understand her dreams, they always showed their support in helping Sarah get to where she wanted to go.

As Sarah emerged into the corporate world, she realized that her business education did not offer her enough on its own to help her succeed. In fact, her business degree gave her the knowledge needed to get the jobs, but it was really her small town values that gave Sarah what she needed to get hired. Because she had been raised to value friendship and community, and to share her services and market her business boldly with the world around her, Sarah learned how to have good business sense.

It was through truly working in New York and acquiring these jobs using the charisma and values that her parents instilled in her that allowed her to truly understand the value of her upbringing. As she was sitting in her corner office admiring the view and eating lunch one day, Sarah realized just how much her parents had contributed to her being able to get to where she was. She realized that if it were not for her small town values, Sarah would have never made the impact she was meant to have in the city. In fact, she may have failed and ended up right back at her parents' house, pursuing something she did not love and living a life that she did not want.

Although her parents did not fully understand, Sarah silently thanked them every single day for raising her in a small town and giving her those values. She no longer resented them for keeping her in that small town and preventing her from living a big city life as a kid. Instead, she was grateful for the entire experience. Sarah still had no desire to move back to the small town that she grew up in, but she did hold it in higher esteem as she realized that it was this small town and her family that had gotten her to where she was, not just her and her schooling.

In life, having values and sharing values is important. When we learn how to care about the things that matter, these core values stay with us for life and they help us in ways we cannot possibly imagine until we are in those situations. There is nothing more valuable than knowing what your own values are and using those values to support you in creating your dream life. So, do not be afraid to dream big and forge a new path for yourself, but also do not forget to honor where you came from and the values that you were taught by the people who raised you.

Chapter 8 Passion

Darlene was a forty-something-year-old woman who had spent her entire life doing everything that she knew she was supposed to do. She woke up every morning at six to feed her dogs and her cat, she made breakfast for her children and her husband, and she fixed a pot of morning coffee. When everyone was fed, she would clean their plates away, tidy up the kitchen, and help everyone get ready for their day. Then, it was off to school. Darlene would then head into the office to work until the school day was over. She would then go pick up her children, bring them home, feed them a snack, and escort them to their after-school activities like soccer, dance, and swim lessons. When everyone got home in the evening, Darlene would fix up a supper, feed everyone, and then clean all of the dishes when everyone was done eating. She would then clean up everyone's book bags and shoes, tidy up any other messes that had been made that day, and then sit down to watch thirty minutes of television before bed. On weekends, Darlene would do all of the same things except instead of going to school or work she would take her kids shopping, to sleepovers, or to their sports events. There was always something going on, and Darlene was always in charge of having to make sure that everything got done in time.

When she was in her early forties, Darlene realized that she was entirely miserable. After spending nearly two decades cleaning up after her family, preparing meals for them, and driving them around everywhere, Darlene realized that she was done. She no longer cared to have the experience of doing everything herself, as it was beginning to take a toll on her. She found that every morning she would wake up depressed and dreading the day before her, and every night she would go to sleep sad and wishing that she could wake up to a brand new life. This brought Darlene great guilt as she loved her family and loved caring for them, though she could no longer do it all by herself.

One day, Darlene was called into her boss's office in the middle of the afternoon. As she got up from her desk and headed toward her boss's office, Darlene tried to recall anything she may have done wrong that could result in her being talked to or written up by her boss. Of course, she could not think of anything she had done wrong as Darlene was always very particular about doing everything properly and by the book. After all, she was great at doing what she knew was expected of her. When she reached her boss's office, Darlene's boss asked her to sit and offered to get her a beverage. Darlene agreed and began sipping on the tea that her boss had brought her as she tried to understand what it was that she had been called in for. To her surprise, Darlene's boss offered her a promotion that came with a substantial raise and increased benefits compared to what she was already receiving. Darlene was excited by the offer, but at the same time, she was miserable to realize that taking it meant that she would be committing to staying in this lackluster life that she was no longer getting joy from. Before she knew what she was doing, Darlene refused the promotion and instead put in her notice and quit her job. She went and cleared out her desk and left, never to look back again.

Darlene's family was surprised to learn that she had quit her job and had no intentions of going back. They were also surprised when she said that she would no longer make breakfast unless she felt like it, that everyone would need to find their own ways to their hangouts, and that the only thing Darlene would help with anymore was getting to sports events or homework. At this point, her kids were old enough that they could walk, bike, or even drive themselves to their own events so she would no longer have to do it. In other words, Darlene was ready to start letting her children grow up and become young adults.

Asserting these boundaries meant that Darlene had great freedom in her life to do whatever it was that she pleased. She could sleep in, eat whenever she wanted, and even watch afternoon television shows that she had heard her friends talking about at the PTA meetings at her children's school for years. Finally, Darlene got what it meant to slow down and just be, rather than to always have to be in motion doing everything in her power to please everyone else.

At first, Darlene's laid back lifestyle was enjoyable like it offered her a great change of pace from what she was used to. Over time, however, it grew boring as she realized that she would always be doing nothing unless she did something to change that. As she did not want to spend her entire life bored, Darlene began looking into different hobbies and discovering new things that she liked. One hobby she found that she was drawn to was making jewelry. Darlene found that not only did she enjoy making jewelry, but also that she was incredibly good at it, and that people often wanted to purchase her jewelry.

Darlene started out making jewelry as a hobby in the afternoons while she watched daytime television. She would make four or five new pieces per week, and inevitably every single piece would sell to someone that she knew. Eventually, she started selling her jewelry online as this gave her the opportunity to sell even more. Before she knew it, Darlene was making copious amounts of jewelry and selling them to friends, family, strangers online, and even stocking it in boutique stores around her town. She grew so excited to make jewelry that Darlene would excitedly get up in the middle of the night and sketch out new plans, or launch from bed in the morning ready to start crafting new creations.

Although it was a far cry from what she was used to, Darlene loved her new life of making and selling handmade jewelry. Her children and husband liked it as well, as they began to realize that Darlene was happier and enjoying life once again. It took them some time to get used to Darlene not being available to help as often anymore, but in the end, they were all happy that Darlene had found her passion and that she was finally enjoying life after helping her family do the very same thing for so many years.

Chapter 9 Trip to an Exotic Resort

Tonight, I am offering you a story about an exotic resort's trip. The days I spent there were luxurious, soothing and comfortable. It was my second time at that resort. I always would like to enjoy here. As an entrepreneur I established my name in the field of healthy food service.

Now, talking about the world's famous Atlantis, The Palm in Dubai: I want you to sit back and relax. With each of the story details you feel deeply relaxed. Lie down on your back and let your feet loosely placed on the base of your bed as the air moves all over your body, your neck, chest, legs and feet are all getting deeper and deeper into the pot of calmness. You are becoming relaxed and relaxed.

I hope you have idea about the glittering state of the United Arab Emirates. It is a combination of all worldly pleasures where skylights strain sky view through crystal clear glasses on the flat rooftops and skywalks are as clear as walking on the natural sky. Imagine, that the sky is visible to you. The sky is above you like a blanket, you are feeling it as comfy as you are gripping pieces of silky fabric in on your chest.

The resort I chose to move in is a combination of top facilities and the never-ending access of deep aqua sea view for your eye candy. Skyscrapers shadow the beach and additionally the access to the inside waterpark and underwater aquarium was free. This freedom is similar to skylines. The Arabian Gulf is breathtaking on the sight as I walked on the hotel's archway. I saw the pink palatial structure all around me. The towers were my neighbors. I felt worthy when I noted the combination of traditional and contemporary touch in my refurbished room with holy terrace at the Jumeirah's island.

It was a distinctive spot for me to discover the soaring turrets. I didn't expect the crescent to be such scenic. I walked to the shower upon this idea because the curiosity to enjoy more flared up within me. I came back into my room and admired the satellite TV besides the minibar. The artificial features of the resort didn't resist me from going out immediately again towards the walkway under the open blue sky. Between the check in and check out of this resort, my arrival and booking for here was the luckiest I could do to myself.

You can imagine this is very secure for you when you are breathing at an exclusive location that you love. All the things that you need are present for relaxing support. You are outside the city's pollution and taking a cool break for holidays at one of the most iconic destinations around the globe. You are digging deeper and deeper into the fabric of your bedding as your base is holding you warmly and comforting you perfectly. You are now more relaxed.

As I headed a few footsteps farther from the main walkway, I scanned the area and found two pools. There were outdoor friendly staff members to host activities. The royal scene of the Dubai cityscape grasped me, as I felt different at every glance of the surroundings. From an award-winning restaurant, the smells of seafood were impressive. The sight of far away land also offered me a view of Ambassador Lagoon and Ossiano that were exclusive for the dining experience with a dress code. I spent a few minutes appreciating the resort's aura and took around to my club double bedroom's balcony for some top view.

Setting back for a moment on a sofa, I changed my clothes from jeans to swimming costumes and made my plan for scuba diving in the open air marine nearby. The opportunity took me to the scuba diving moves by a dolphin in that largest pool. You know you can also choose the diving courses to get trained under the supervision of certified divers. It was safe not only for adults but children too. I saw the terraces of suits from a tower at the back of the diving site where people were enjoying the rain that continued for a few minutes. I am glad that I have a chance to share the breathtaking relaxation that rain supplied. I ate delicious food recommended by the resort's manager and remained comfortable until the next morning.

After incredible scuba diving in front of the resort, it had been absolutely amazing to take some time around other facilities of the palm facing the open sky on the 21ST floor. I was deep breathing as I looked upon the marina street festival. It was the 10TH March and remembers that it's the day of my father's birthday. As I went downstairs to closely enjoy the troupe of entertainers in the costumes of clowns and acrobats beside the mall. As I gathered the details of the mall timings I was in search of some own private time alone at the beach's sand. The entire sand was welcoming me as I sat on one of the seating and spread my legs, sunbathe was kissing me hard. I must say that I didn't want to come back to the resort's room for leaving anywhere else.

The white sand beaches are the best out there. I took more relaxed air into my lungs. You feel completely relaxed when all the green palm trees are bowing in a row to you. You are sliding into your pillow with an extreme and deeply relaxed state of mind and body. Your hips are rested on a sheet and soft mattress fibers are felt closer to you. Waterfront buildings are seemed full of youth. Stars are pouting behind the clouds and public is sipping exotic cocktails in colorful glasses. Atlantis's fresco bar arms are wide open to embrace you. Walk-in showers are installed with sea view and an air-conditioned room with limited area to get dressed is accessible.

Let your fingers linger upon your chest and in slow motion, keep your hands resting on your thighs. Make your thighs straight and legs relaxed. As you are getting deeper and deeply relaxed, I am continuing to describe the glory of the resort. Close your eyes softly and visualize with me. You can easily feel that your mind runs imagination about the peace upon the sky by drawing own thoughts away out of your awareness.

Within the next 4 minutes as I touched my king size bed, I was ready to sleep on my day 1 in Dubai's resort. The last thought I had about my room that night was everything was arranged with French art. My neighbor room's guest was checking in when I left the room and a glimpse of their queen size bed remind me of my previous visit at this resort. Anyhow, today I had the route to the private beach, some other pools and their nightclub in the last. Upon entering the lobby I was impressed by the shops in front of the large hall. The hall was similar to what we visualize from the Disney movies and the collection at the shops was mind-blowing. Due to placement in the Emirates, the lobby shops were as huge as the malls have. The traditional and modern touches of items within each shop were flattering. I bet anyone who visited there must go back to their homes emptied of money and the cash they had when they joined in here. Same I can say about the nightlife in Dubai. I cannot even choose which of these was my favorite activity. But I can describe that I became fit as I was served with fitness and spa services daily to get rid of lethargy.

You are just fine on a fluffy couch. Your hands are held with softness as if the feathers are slightly moving on your skin. You are resting with your eyes closed and eyelids tightly secured when your feet are dipped into lukewarm water with a smell of rose and rosewater is sprinkled on your face to suck off the pollutants and misery. As they apply some warmth on your legs' muscles you are feeling above the sky, flying higher without any fear. Your worries are now thrown in a waste bag to the dustbin.

What destiny! I trust that destiny brings me here. Spending some moments outside the walls are priceless. The soft air was giving me a pleasurable kiss. Admiring this resort, I learned some of the historical facts from the manager out there. He told me about how it was established 11 years ago. Two of the tycoons in Dubai gave a thought on this project and they contributed their property at stake with a 50% share of each of them. This information was as enjoyable as living in a resort. I was holding my cup of herbal tea that was prepared from the fresh herbal plants they have planted in the resort area. The smell of chamomile was like an illusion for me.

Continuing what else the manager had to say, I was taking sips from the warm cup merrily and I was literally feeling that my day's fatigue shed the skin of my body. A firm specialized in working for luxurious hotels planned the architect of the resort. After, a multinational constructor started to stand the phases of the resort. It took no longer to officially announce it open. The fireworks were illuminated and all the artificial lighting was used that displayed a show of lights onto the rooftop. They also stated that a million of them were used in that show and for 15 minutes, they were displayed almost seven times.

This was the short story of the grand opening ceremony. Just imagine, the resort all lit up and full of crowd stretched from 400 balconies. The status of this hotel even rose when someone found a mermaid in the front beach after this discovery they assembled bottlenose dolphins from an island to create an environment of fantasy like a place for visitors. The shocking news was that the government took serious steps for the care of the resort and hotel facilities after the popularity between the whole United Arab Emirates. I can understand why is it so, it worth this attention.

Now, was the time for testing diversity? Yes, you hear this right. Taste from all over the world was exhibited there. I was almost lost to think about what to try and what to leave for the next visit. Let me tell you one by one. There was a set in a pavilion full of gardens and a pool where beauty and body treatments were offered using Malay products and healing experts. They claimed that all your dead skin and scars would be removed within 25 minutes of intense rubbing on the affected area.

I hope you get an idea of what you are about to receive further. The resort treatments next included the healing with a waterfall view that was artificial but the exciting and humorous element was you have to dip your feet in a tub full of tiny fishes. And that fishpond had its own benefits to treat your body issues. I dared to pour my hands for some time but I quitted the idea to expose my facial skin.

I was adding the stuff to my memories with versatile benefits. A lust garden was present in the center of these treatment tents spread on 1000s of square meters but separated by little ponds with fresh lilies. Again, I imagine the fairytales like a view in the middle of a heavenly spa that was nestled with windows to appreciate the location where these services were waiting for people like us. We are the kind of carefree and full of life. I have been a lover of luxury since childhood.

Close your eyes and feel the deeply relaxed muscles of your face, hands, fingers and hips. You are going into a deeply relaxed posture. Your limbs are very light and you are laid straight with your muscles relaxed. Now you are getting even more relaxed with every moment. Your body is calmer and mind is deeply relaxed. Keeping your eyes closed you are peaceful as if you are in a spa. The softness of a masseur hands is soothing you. You are getting deeper and deeper into the state of calmness. Now, you are more, and more relaxed.

I was picking interesting things out there to try for enjoyment, as I perceived the boards, I read "barefoot" that was the name for another spectacular spa. This was not the last, I also observed some of the romantic spas with hammocks inside to enjoy, chat and get treated with your couple. The Southeast Asian style spa was typically rough with excellent services and experts to transfer their civilization in a different manner. I am sure I was not alone who had a hard time deciding about the services to try, anyone who visits there will experience the same.

Till the evening, I gathered hours of pleasurable treatments blast I ooze out like a liquid from there towards the sand. The sand was absorbing, affectionate and in the evening it held me like a child. I found myself on the sand sitting firm to take a glance of overwater bungalows at one side in the east. The direction of those accommodations sounded well protected. You are on 24 hours leave and you are going more and more into a relaxed state of mind. Your body is loose from the limbs, abdomen, chest, shoulders, and neck. You have released all your tensions and your weight is totally thrown on your bed. You are comfortable in your skin and suit. You are the one who has nothing to think about for the next few hours. You are free to rest longer and longer.

The resort looked like a maze and made its way for attention. It was designed so well in the first glance and in the next glance it had arcs to take ways towards different places. Tunnels and fountains presented on the edges of the horizon of the resort were strings to the connection between two areas within the resort. The blue pools and beachside were the most suitable parts of the landscapes. They were like swimming bars, long and wide beneath the orchids where you can stare for long to the beauty of the surface. On about 100 meters, tiles were floored in a mosaic pattern with diamond print on the canopies. Can you think of these million dollars idea for covering rooftops? The setting demands for clapping in that resort. That was perfect for a private lifestyle and appeal all those who need time alone on their own. They also incorporated alluring villas and living styles brought from grassland countries. Time runs, as I was busy in fetching details. You are getting slower and slower, lazier and lazier when there is so much peace, comfort, breeze and warmth in the temperature that you want to kiss the ceilings and like to swim on floors.

The region was broad and I was in need of boasting my trip memories through diary notes and pictures. There was no escape from the magic of the blended place with the indigenous setting. After the next 18 hours, I had my flight back to hometown in England from this room in UAE where I was checked in the resort. I was calmly waiting in a private sauna for a masseur to give massage softly as a token of goodbye from that place to me. This last treatment was also given as a featured facility beside an outdoor living area. I saw a whirlpool at few steps in a villa and I fell in love with the cliffs that were crashing as the waves come down from the higher tidal activity. The overwhelming feeling melted and encouraged me to happily write a farewell speech in a few words for the blogging I love to do. With new leaps, I always inspire the world to drip over such resorts and sightseeing once a year for sure. You can drag all stress away from you and seek the stunning blue water's loving dose or inhale views under the Jacuzzis' round the clock at your customized pleasure zones.

I have bought some very useful oils namely spearmint and turmeric from a herbal relaxation shop because I wanted to soothe myself when I go back to routine and exercise I will be using them to rest my tight and tense body. For a week after I returned to my home from the outstanding place, I was feeling overall fantastic. You are satisfied as if you have been given a remote control to open the doors of blessings. Imagine a magic key to a magic space is now in your hands. As you enter into that space you are feeling light, clean and easy. Your eyes are getting heavier and demands rest. You are in a big room on a bed full of direct fresh breeze. On dusty weather you are compelled to weave the wonderful dreams that imperial staff of the palm is giving you a hot tender rub on your forehead and you are going beyond the light of consciousness. Go deeper and deeper in the depths of the most affectionate charm and stay there.

Take a deep breath one more time. You are now moving to a deeper state of relaxation. Your upper arms are straight and in relaxed position, your whole body is relaxed even you are feeling that from your head to the toes, there is calmness spread within you. You are feeling that now you have a very soothing and calm body. Your muscles are very relaxed and you are getting more and more relaxed state of mind. Now, as you are very peaceful you are becoming relaxed, relaxed, relaxed, relaxed, relaxed.

Chapter 10 Harvesting Site For Fruits

I am taking you to a faraway land in Italy, where my uncle has a fruit farm. This farm is the harvesting site of Joseph Smith, my father's younger brother. In rainy weather, I chose to visit him last October. I welcome you to the farm with my uncle and me.

Lay down on your bed. Straighten your shoulders. Close your eyes and let your arms and legs spread straight to feel a deep relaxation. You are going to feel an extreme calmness. Visualize the starry night above your head and a bed of roses at the base of your back. You are going deeper now as you are getting absorbed in the center of candles dim light aroma. You are getting more and more relaxed in an airy environment.

I can see the blurry air and the dusty floor, a road that goes straight to the harvesting area. I reached in the evening at the site to spend the next complete day on the farm because his house is quite far away in the main city and the farm is outside the district. He has a small guesthouse within the site and I ate dinner and sleep due to extreme tiredness. You can sense the proper presence of trees and sweet aroma that flies toward you with a solid and outstanding quality of the soil that you can feel within the surroundings. It is like rolling on the floor full of soil like a child and absorbing the soothing unseen particles.

It was magical. I am a fan of nature but harvesting and packing related topics fantasize me equally. Indeed it is obvious that I am lusty for the juice-filled soft and mushy fruits. Each drop of flesh that fruits provide makes me appreciate the countless flavors and smells they contain. The fruits attainment process needs proper time, knowledge of seeds and plants. This is one of the botanical ventures whose desire is governed by the passion for storage and protection of various related products.

The consumption of fruits takes a few minutes. The fruits are sold within hours as well. It can be stored for weeks or months. The frozen fruits spend a season in a good state, for example, you can freeze them for a year and it stays fresh and pure. The time of fruits harvesting is similar to the time when they are eaten. Usually, we see that pears and bananas are harvested and they are consumed during the same period in ripen or immature forms. The state of some outstanding foods does not make any difference. People eat them and satisfy their taste pallets as well as to attain a considerable amount of nutritive value.

There are many other examples of common fruits that I can give you. My uncle and I talked about citric fruits category for an hour and I took notice that we can store many varieties of avocados, oranges, and grapefruits for months and even we can leave them without any issue for several months on the trees on which they grow. Upon close observation, I found that they are naturally of good quality when right procedures are applied to grow them and care we provide in handling and packaging for transport also has a role in marketing costs of these fruits.

Imagine the fingertips of your loved one closing your eyes and your eyelashes are smoothly touching the portion under your eyes. You are going deeper and deeper in a calming state of mind. There is so much peace and relaxation when you loosely place your arms on the grass under a tree.

You must be waiting to listen to some other facts about the exotic lemons, apples and a bunch of other flavors. They are dissimilar than those we discussed before, as they tend to drop off from the tree after complete maturation. Uncle told me that when fruits start to drop before the maturation period, this is called pre-harvest drop. They control this problem with a chemical spray particularly used to apply on such fruit trees in order to help them in growth regulation for a considerable time period. It takes normally 4-6 weeks after blooming.

It was very interesting for my senses and taste buds when I tasted a small pear and took advantage of fully ripe fruit. There are many other advantages of eating fully ripen fruits directly taken from a harvesting fruit farm. The natural growth without any substances pollution is not only reducing the digestive period but also supply all the naturally occurring nutrients located just beneath the skin. I have no idea why but I picked an apple and took a bite after washing it simply with cold tap water. The bite was rich and heavenly as I am invited on a seasonal fruit festival.

I forgot all the fruits that I have been buying to eat from the local markets near my residence in Bulgaria, Germany. I was sunken into the memories of my childhood when my siblings joined me for summer vacations with uncle's family and we were served with these farm fresh fruits as a treat. As I came out of my emotional flashback while taking the last bite of the small apple I picked a few moments ago I saw my uncle at some distance who was harvesting the bush fruits by hand as he used to do years back when he was younger. Even in childhood, our favorite day to celebrate in Italy was the day of our visit to the uncle's fresh fruit farm and harvesting site.

Imagine a fruit is just dropped from tree to the hay and softly it sunk into it and mixed with soil. The soil folded the red apple's skin. This gradual mechanical motion of fruit dropping down is similar to you going deeper into the sleeping area. This process is driven automatically. Your motor movements have stopped just like the apple becomes stagnant once it touched the ground.

Place your hands on your abdomen. Now, as you are getting more and more relaxed you are feeling deep calmness. Your muscles from upper body to lower body are relaxed. You are going into a deep relaxation position. Your limbs are relaxed, your neck muscles are relaxed and you are laid on your back with deep relaxation.

Occasionally I watched the bush shakers that were attached to the trees appropriately with the use of belts. These tricks were labor-saving plans and a replacement of artificial intelligence machines largely growing these days. Still, our family does not like to take risks and prevent fruits from possible harm through traditional ways of picking little gifts with hands. This is also better for saving the good appearance of the fruit in order to earn more profits from and for suppliers and store managers. These characteristics push the fruits in best grade and its availability increases for the public so that growers have more benefits.

They call the process of attaining ripened fruits, the senescence. When they reach the final developmental stage they are signified as the fleshy ovary of a flower. Sometimes we see the ripening of fruits in the floral parts of the tree in the case of my favorite apples, pineapples, and pears. The cells multiply through pollination or the phases of fertilization and stimulate the rapid growth of fruits for us. The science of fruits harvesting is very satisfactory. Within this one cycle that we can apply on all fruits, we find different structures of fruits for example how lemons are different from apples.

The formation of the young cells of fruits is identified by ingredient protoplasm that is filled in the cells. This demands the use of plant hormones to expand the young cells to transfer it from embryonic seeds readily to bigger size and weight. Like the reproduction system of all living organisms in this life, we can relate the harvesting and growth of the fruit with how we accumulate some life to the tissues of the organisms. In fruits, small spaces called vacuolated that is derived as cavities are the center of attention. From here foodstuff originates.

This is a breathtaking experience that how diverse the fruits are in their compositions and not only appearance.

The dates, bananas, and apples have mainly high content of carbohydrates while the olives and avocados are composed of fatty acids that are stored in the form of nutrients to benefit us, heal us and enrich our body and minds. Citric acid is found in pineapples and oranges this reason they are recognized as citrus fruits. They are the valuable constituents of nature's magic. However, for some good reason, we don't get proteins in fruits. By fruits intake, we receive tartaric acid as in grapes and malic acid as in pears, apples, and similar tree fruits.

You see that some fruits are gone through maturation stages in green color. This state is also seen in markets especially in guavas, bananas. Green color colored apples are also used widely as edible products. You are fantasized by the dramatic changes of fruits that sound familiar because you have been enjoying the softening of sugary fruits between your teeth. The moment you take a bite from one of your preferred fruits, it melts and disappears into your digestive system through your throat. The food pipe is smoothly sliding it and you are greatly thankful for this refreshment for the next few minutes till the taste of the fruit is on your tongue and smell is perceived by your brain.

Fruits are of an attractive character. There is no doubt that cell walls substance called chlorophyll diminishes over time from the background of fruits. They are the same material that gives the green color pigmentation just before the ripening state. The pigments of carotenoids that give a yellow-orange hue to the fruits and anthocyanins that give red color to the berries and mangoes replace the green state following the disappearance of the substance. Usually, acidic foods drop down in their acidic content and rise in sweetness due to high sugar content at this stage. They are the real causes behind your love for the fruits and the sensory pleasure they have to shift to us. You might agree to my observation that frequent changes in the composition of fruits verify that they are short-lived and perishable. Temporary they can be kept without any protective measures i.e. freeze state. In the long run, distinct lovely aroma also expires leaving the fruits. The phenomenon is the same for climate bound kinds of fruits including the pears and not for berries and cherries as non-climacteric fruit.

You must admire the flattery of fruits growing process with me. How beautifully they turn into molecules of bliss. The enzymatic activity gradually reacts to bring up the catalytic result in the form of products to seek soothing and calm layer of fruit's skin, sensual fleshy juice, and bits of other feeding chunks. You are experiencing excellence in the dry and liquid source of vitamins and minerals. Your skin is relaxed, your face is relaxed and even your fiery palates are going into intense exposure to cool effect.

Take a long deep breath. Your senses are calming down. Your nerves are now getting more and more relaxed. Now, you are even deeply relaxed and relaxed. As your muscles are all relaxed you are going deeper and deeper in even more peaceful posture.

Prior to the harvesting stuff, it is very essential to know that when to harvest the most nutritious and tastiest fruits. To ensure the time of harvest, a visual and textual clues guide is helpful. The over-ripening and picking time is also decided in a similar manner. To avoid picking fruits before they ripen, I learn harvesting time hints from my uncle. The netting is the first sign for cantaloupes. We discussed that the surface is covered with beige to green shade on the fruit. This looks a bit under pressure with a sweet smell that indicates that fruit is ready for a slight pull and this easily stems out afterward.

He then shared the warning signs for harvesting melons. This fruit is the only one that is harvested just before few days of the fully ripen shape appearance. Before you reach your hands on the full ripeness of the fruit on a tree, you can feel the harvesting period has arrived as you penetrate your fingernail into the watermelon. They turn cream or yellow and give a resonant sound as you tap on the skin. When you store that at room temperature, in a couple of days the taste becomes completely sweet.

Pears have a longer timeframe with indoors access for consumption. You allow it to start spoiling if they were picked fully ripen. However, to check the harvest time for them you can simply place them under a specific temperature. Then keep on looking with ripeness test of applying thumb pressure on its neck every day. For long-term storage, use refrigeration. We also talked about apples, cherries, strawberries and blueberries and different varieties of fruits. The principles are present to follow for each stage of maturation, storage, and quality check.

Experts define the lifespan details for fruits and vegetables. They share them in terms of shape, skin color and optical methods. Assessment of the fruit ripening properties is seen in the form of light transmission measurement. The transfer is seen through chlorophyll II content in total darkness. There are many other advanced methods like caliber check for size in the maturity of fruits for grading purposes. Other factors that matter are aroma and openings as they are synthesized volatile chemicals and human beings need to detect them for commercial purposes. Leaf quality changes in the fruit plants and firmness also give a signal for root crops.

The juice content in fruit is another standard that is measured in proportion to the minimum value settled for this purpose compared with the original mass of the fruit. In a specific manner, these indicators are of big help in the mature citrus identification. To carry out all this, containers are needed in the field. The crops are picked in bags usually to sling on the shoulders and waist. Workers take care of the fruits and handle within containers. The workers who work in these fields are agricultural carriers. They are common transports the fruit within the field in woven baskets. There is less risk of contamination and they are also recommended for protection to retain the fruits in their actual position.

When it comes to the packaging section I saw the small wood pulps to hold them as the base and supporting layers of the fruits. The positioning is in a way that one fruit doesn't apply pressure on any other. Some of them are placed within plastic foams and clean paper covers so that they are sealed with polythene films and heat bags based on the climatic condition. In one layer they almost settle 4-6 pieces. This is a popular way of delivering these yummy fruits from this farm. The harvested fruits of one kind hold almost a few dozen of them at a time.

I tried packing apples and citrus using the same method to avoid bruising of the fruits until they reach their distribution destinations. On this farm, we also sold loose fruits in trays with a firm fitting film of plastic. Meanwhile, we waited for the trucks to pick the packets of fruits to pull in the containers one by one to take away from here. To deal with atmospheric problems tight containers are sometimes used for refrigeration whenever required for the elimination of fruit growth retardation. Another way that my uncle uses to transport fruits for distribution to sell them is the air shipment. Beautifully packed fruits increasingly supply within a short time through this means. Faster cargo is more profitable because it takes care of larger amounts of fruits within a short time.

There are certain temperatures to store the fruits and eat them fresh after a long time if they are secure in suitable and secure material of containers. We must use them after proper washing and cleaning until we see the shine on the skin of the fruits. The pest control and decay spray effect must shed off before the use of this delicious mini treat. The sour and sweet, they have a combination of parts within them.

I collected all the fruits in a basket to place them in the storage area and took rest for 30 minutes. Before we left the site we ate special chunks from the mixed fruit table prepared by one of the workers, they carefully cut and decorate the fruits to help us fill our appetite and to feel good with a number of flavors. We enjoyed, cleaned our mouths and thanked them for the memorable food. We were tired and full of sightseeing at the same time. We still chat about how we worked at the farm for a whole day. I missed that place a lot.

You smell such bliss whenever you are close to fruit from the vine or tree. Distance doesn't matter to inhale the sweetness of the juicy and nutritious fruits. The colors are playing with your vision and you are losing consciousness as if the fruits are pampering your whole body with their properties to ease the tension and providing relief to your mind and body. You are appreciating the texture of floral thin fiber spreads that are pulling the flowers out of it to prepare fruits. You are now more and more relaxed as your upper body muscles are resting and lower body is loosely thrown as you lay straight on a comfortable base of silky bedding to give you the grassy appeal on the skin covering your backbone. As your back touches the slightly cold grass like velvety base, you are now digging into the allure of fruits deeper and deeper. You are becoming relaxed, relaxed, relaxed, relaxed and relaxed.

Chapter 11 Dandelion Wish

The summer was as gorgeous as any Jenny had known.

Days of running through the sprinklers, and going out to the lake, and having picnics in the local park.

Roasting marshmallows in the fire pit out in the backyard, making s'mores, and enjoying family get-togethers around the barbecue.

The weather was warm but cold lemonade and shade under the trees helped to keep everyone cool.

Jenny worked hard and brought about many changes: remodeling the home, taking on a new role at work, helping her daughter recover from her very first exciting school year.

Tonight, Jenny sat with Kirsty out by the fire pit in the fading evening light.

The others had gone inside, but she wanted to spend the night with her daughter and enjoy one of the last nights of summer.

The smell of wood smoke drifted on the air. Gentle pops and crackles accompanied the embers that floated up in the air, glimmered, and went out.

One of Jenny's favorite things in the whole world was to sit next to a fire and enjoy the warmth and flickering glow, and the sound, the smell, all of it. She loved it, and now she had passed that down to her daughter, as well.

The steady sound of crickets and the occasional hoot of a night bird made a relaxing chorus to lull their heavy eyelids ever down further.

"I want a story, Mom," said Kirsty, yawning heavily in her chair. Then she hugged the blanket she had brought outside even closer around her.

Her head leaned back, but she was not ready yet. Jenny had brought out a sleeping bag because sometimes they liked to sleep out under the stars, on perfect nights like tonight.

Kirsty got out of her chair, went over to the sleeping bag, and slid into it, the fabric swishing loudly as she snuggled in.

Jenny moved her chair over near the sleeping bag.

"I thought you might, honey, so I came prepared!"

Jenny lifted the book she had had sitting beside the chair: their favorite storybook.

"How are you going to read in the dark, Mommy?"

The flickering firelight did not offer much steady light for reading, but Jenny only smiled.

"Oh, don't worry, baby."

She opened the book and turned to one of the summer chapters, and a golden light spilled out from the very pages, illuminating Jenny is smiling face.

"This one creates its own light. And it is a good thing, too! We're going to see a lot and we need lots of good light for this one!"

The pages showed a field of dandelions basking in the sunlight. Thousands of yellow flowers upon a deep green canvas.

A single slender creek ran through the field of green and yellow, forming a sort of S-curve, or maybe like a stylized numeral "5."

Jenny held up the book to show her daughter, whose eyes grew wide and her smile—missing a tooth and all—grew even wider.

"That looks like such a nice place, Mom! Can we go there someday?"

Jenny grinned and put the book back in her lap. She turned the page with the creaking of thick, glossy paper and said, "Sweetie, we're going to go there right now! Just imagine the scent of the flowers...."

* * *

Jaina ran barefoot through the dandelion fields.

Soft grass and cold, moist dandelions comforted her feet as she ran, springing up again as she passed through.

Other flowers stood amid the dandelions but she loved them all equally. There were white flowers and pink and blue ones, all set against the deepest green grass, and the dandelions shone like droplets fallen from the sun on high.

The smell was so divine! Aromatic grass, wild and thick, met with the fragrances of sweet nectar.

Breathing it in was like feeling the soft petals gently caressing her face. Jaina could never get tired of it.

She knelt down and scooped a fuzzy white dandelion out of the earth. Holding it aloft, some of the seeds began to blow away on the wind.

Jaina watched them float, and she laughed because that was exactly what she wanted to wish for.

"I wish I could fly as you do, and see what you see!"

Then she pursed her lips and blew, scattering all but one seed from the dandelion head.

Before she moved on, she returned the plant to the ground and scooped dirt over its roots again.

The wind tugged at that last remaining parachute seed until it, too, floated away…right past Jaina's hand.

She reached out as if to catch it, and then she found herself swept up in the breeze.

The world swirled upward as she rose, hanging on to the dandelion seed, now grown to giant size.

No, wait, maybe she had shrunk so much that it was like a parachute carrying her across the meadow. Vivid colors blended into a living painting, stretching as far as the horizon.

Countless flowers waved in the breeze, each a little point of light, like a star in a deep emerald sky. About them wove beautiful music, thousands upon thousands of voices raised up together in song.

The wind whooshed and the dandelion seed soared as the ground fell away in rolling hills. She lifted higher into the sky, where winds flowed like river currents in an invisible ocean.

The sky darkened. Something passed by overhead, giving out a proud cry.

It was an eagle, soaring with its feathers in the sun. Jaina beamed as she looked up at it.

She had always loved birds, admired their freedom in flight, and now she has to experience the same thing.

The dandelion seed caught an updraft and higher she went still, hot on the tail of the mighty eagle.

Floating beside it, she laughed, and tears streamed from her face, in sheer joy.

This was something she had always wanted, and now her wish had come true!

The eagle looked over at her with a gleam in his golden eye. "Hello, stranger!" he said. "You wish to fly under the summer sun as I do?"

Jaina's heart leaped. "Yes! This is a wish come true, Mr. Eagle!"

The eagle's eyes turned back to the horizon. If it was possible, somehow a smile lifted the corners of his beak. "Then would you like to fly with me for a while? Just let go and I will bear you."

Jaina's eyes were round with awe. She looked up at the fluffy white dandelion seed.

"See you soon, okay? Don't forget me!"

And she let go, the seed obligingly floating along beside the eagle for a moment as he swooped lower and Jaina landed on his head.

Clinging to one feather, she shaded her eyes and found that she could see as the eagle saw.

Blue Mountains appeared out of what was a haze in the distance, rising and falling like distant waves.

Each flower she saw in clarity even from so high up, their petals glowing in the sun.

Trees rose like spires from the land, each holding an entire world in their branches.

The eagle saw all: the scurrying squirrels and the nesting birds, the hares and the deer, the fish gleaming in the far-away streams winding about the feet of the trees.

Here, this place was alive with the fullness of the summer, an inexhaustible flame of vitality.

Beyond the green and growing things, the eagle saw the spirits of land and sky, which frolicked as happily as a bird on the wing.

They were tiny like Jaina, or big like the eagle, sometimes both at once. Their lives mirrored that of the land itself.

Where they trod, life bloomed, and where life bloomed, they gravitated, forever finding meaning in the growth of the smallest seed, or the tranquility of the tallest tree.

Jaina realized that even during the day, when most were wide-awake and stretching out beneath the sun, the world dreamed, and she floated through its dreams at once an observer and a fellow traveler.

She breathed in deeply as the wind rushed across her face, granting her a sense of freedom she had never know before.

Here, sailing upon the sky itself, she knew what the golden days of late summer meant to all that lived within them.

She could feel the vibrant pulse of the world hot in her veins. It gave her such a sense of purpose, an invigoration that nothing else could match.

"You must not forget this feeling," said the eagle.

"This is life, my friend. Life at its purest. Enjoying sun, star, and moon. Breathing in the wind. Flying freely. You could weigh as much as a tree and still not burden me, for I am free. Here you are free, too."

A rocky outcropping stood tall over the bank of a wide blue lake below.

The eagle dipped his head. "Farewell, friend! Return whenever it pleases you!"

Jaina dove from the eagle's head turned and waved goodbye to him as she fell.

She spread her arms and let the wind slip through her fingers, cool and soft.

The lake grew as she fell toward it, but she was not afraid. Like a drop of rain, she broke the surface and plunged into another world.

The lake welcomed her as it welcomed the sunlight, which cast rays that soon became swirling mist within the waves.

And in the water's cold, refreshing embrace she saw more travelers. Big, silvery fish, their eyes bigger than her sprite-sized body, swam past, lazily enjoying the warm waters.

Jaina found that she could move through the water as freely as the eagle had the air, and she glided over to a bed of kelp that grew outward like a swaying forest.

A soft song like a hum rose from the kelp, celebrating its perspective: a green plant that enjoyed both water and sun in equal measure.

Jaina reached out and touched one of the leafy stalks and for a moment saw what the kelp saw: an entire kingdom stretching out across the bottom of the lake, and a sky ever shimmering at the surface.

Fish hid within its leafy mass. Crawdads crawled across the silt within its reach. Frogs and tadpoles danced to its endless tune. Ducks in the water sent ripples ringing like notes across the wave-sky above.

Pieces of driftwood floated by and some of the kelp would seize onto it, pulled free to drift with the wood.

The kelp saw all these lives bound together by the water and the growing earth and the sweet air above. Its perspective was truly blessed, to know so much of the lake's grand symphony.

Jaina swam back to the surface, buoyed by the haze of sunlight filtering down through the water.

She surfaced, listening to the plink and splash of the water.

Jaina lay back and closed her eyes, floating like a flower petal and simply enjoying the relaxing sounds.

She slept, or perhaps sleeping was the same as waking here, where dream and reality were one.

When she opened her eyes, no time had passed at all. The sun was still high in the sky above the lake, and a warmth rippled across the water.

Her breathing coincided with the rise and fall of the gentle waves. In, the water rose, lifting her toward the sky. Out, the water sank, and she felt cradled in a cool liquid bed.

In. Out. A year could have rolled past and she was so calm she would have never noticed it.

Presently a deep hum beat the air. Jaina opened her eyes.

A dragonfly hovered over the lake surface nearby, landing on a small piece of driftwood.

To the rest of the world, it was only a few inches long, but to Jaina the traveler, it looked to be closer in size to an actual dragon!

"Hello!" she called, waving. The dragonfly turned its head to her and its wings buzzed.

"Hello. Fine day, is it not?"

"Yes, it is!" Jaina clapped, incredibly amused that the dragonfly had answered her. "I have never enjoyed the lake so much."

The dragonfly buzzed in agreement. "Oh yes. The sun is pleasant and the water is refreshing. But I must be going. Will you need a lift?"

Jaina's eyes lit up.

"Could I?" She reached out, and the dragonfly lifted off, hovering over to her, and reached down one of its many hands to clasp hers.

Then the dragonfly laughed. "Do hold on!" With a humming whoosh, he was off and they flew above the lake, where leaves traveled on the wind and massive birds beat the air with their wings.

The dragonfly wove through it all skillfully, his wings ever humming like an endless guitar note.

Jaina looked down at the lake slowly strolling past beneath her, an amazing view of its shimmering surface from high up.

Never before had she had such a perfect wish granted?

A white cloud descended to fly next to her—no, not a cloud, the dandelion seed.

The very same one, she was sure of it.

"Thank you!" she called to the dragonfly before she let go and took hold of the floating seed again.

"May the winds bear you to wherever your heart desires!" called the dragonfly, and then he flew back down toward the lakeshore.

But Jaina floated upward and upward, the lake shrinking beneath her.

Soon she plunged into the clouds, rolling white mountains of mist and magic.

Jaina saw shapes therein: faces, animals, trees, castles. She saw glistening streams of water spiraling through the clouds like the dreams of rain. Cool moisture kissed her skin, warmed again by the sun when they emerged into the open blue air.

Jaina had never tasted such pure, sweet air, tinged with the scent of a fresh-fallen rain.

When the sunbeams hit the clouds just the right way they glittered like a field of stars.

Then one of the clouds would break and a torrent of rain fell, shining colors like stained glass as it poured down to the earth. Each raindrop was a different note and created the perfect symphony of sun and sky as she listened.

The dandelion seed passed through a wisp of cloud and Jaina, lulled nearly to sleep, let go.

She waved. "Farewell! Thank you for letting me fly with you!"

The seed floated slowly away, vanishing into the clouds, where its own dreams had always taken it.

Jaina lay back in a bed of pure softness, white like snow, warm like a lake in the sun, and clear as the air after a cleansing rainstorm. She spread her arms wide and closed her eyes.

A soft sound like the sighing of wind mingled with the gentle slosh of lake water filled all her mind.

Then she grew content, more so than she had ever known, freed as the wind and water, birds and clouds, from the burdens of her daily stresses.

Jaina slept in a sea of clouds and the smile never left her lips.

On a Mountain Top

From the mountain top, I look out and this is what I see

A tiny town, and a river running through the valley

Long wild grasses and multi-colored wildflowers grew all around

I felt the heartbeat of the earth when I placed my hand upon the ground

I could tell at once that this was some sort of scared space

And that my footprints should be the only thing I left in this place

The birds sang from hidden spots in the ancient trees

Their song, grew more riveting as it was accompanied by the bumblebees

Foxes played and yipped in the forest, hidden from view

Rabbits danced and jumped encircled in a field of bamboo

The old tribes called this place The Mountain of the Eagle

Trees, older than the oldest man reach to the sky, and stones stand tall and regal

From this mountain top, I hear the voices of the generations past

I know that I must preserve this hallowed spot so that it will last

A Summer Night

The Air is full of expectation

The Sun burns hot in anticipation

Summer is close at hand

Natures fertility fills the land

Time for dancing and light

Sacred dancing through the night

Come jump over a fire

And wish for what it is that you desire

All fae folk gather in the wood

Singing "All of nature is good"

Frolicking upon the Earth Mother

Call her name Gaia or any other

Dance before the waterfall

Singing, dancing and merry-making one and all

Young faeries giggle under a flowering tree

A summer night; and all are free

The Lake

In the summer, the lake is my playground

In winter, I enjoy it when the tourists leave town

In spring, its surface is like reflective glass

In the autumn, the whitecapped waves crash

The lake is a place for fun and play

Or for celebrating Independence Day

The lake changes from season to season

I love it for this very reason

Living at the lake all of the time

Is, I must say, completely sublime

There is nothing quite like my little cabin on the lake

In every season, from heatwave to snowflake

The Dog Days of Summer

The dog days of summer are upon us

Heat radiates off every surface

The only relief is a lawn chair in the share

And a nice, tall glass of lemonade

A cooling breeze is nowhere to be found

Thank goodness, ice cream trucks abound

Playing their happy tune as they go along

Every kid in the neighborhood is chasing that song

The air is so hot and hazy

Such days as this were made for being lazy

A siesta, it seems is in part of the plan

Laying in the sun, getting a tan

Dandelion Journey

Once I took a journey upon a dandelion seed

In was the most magical ride indeed

First, I shrank until I was two inches tall

I grabbed ahold of a seed, a bit afraid of a fall

But soon I was aloft and riding the breeze

And away I went, as fanciful as you please

I traveled over many a meadow and field

And once by one, the secret places were revealed

I happened across a hidden butterfly glade

And watched as the fluttered in sunshine and shade

I hovered above the tree where the bees keep their hives

All of the workers, so busy to ensure their queen survives

And then I voyaged to the place where a young deer spent her day

Secretly nestled in the tall grasses where her mother left her to play

Watching over, in the branches of a tree, a bluebird did chatter

His eagle eye alerting the mother when something is the matter

And then, I arrived back at my home, all too soon

Back to normal, with the memories of a magical afternoon

If you ever get a chance to make a wish on a dandelion

Ask for a dandelion journey and soon you will be high flyin'

Cloud Gazing

Laying upon the summer grass, gazing into the clouds I see

A dog, a dinosaur and a 50-foot bumblebee

I have spent many a summer days

Staring into the sky, even though the late summer haze

The breeze blows and the hours pass me by

And still, I lay here looking up at the sky

Fluffy clouds tell stories one by one

From the first morning light until the day is done

Then comes in a strong breeze

That sends my clouds running, fast as you please

And when each marshmallow cloud has blown away

I shall smile remembering their playful display

Chapter 12 Autumn Dreams

Jenny shook her head in dismay as she looked at her child, sitting amid a veritable pile of candy wrappers.

A cold Autumn breeze rolled in through the window and she got up to shut it.

"What am I going to do with you, kiddo? You are going to be up all night, bouncing off the walls with all that sugar! What was I thinking?"

Kirsty literally bounced on the bed, her gap-toothed grin fueled by entirely too much chocolate and marshmallow.

"Best Halloween ever, Mommy! I got, like, a hundred pounds of candy!"

Jenny laughed. The girl's enthusiasm was, if nothing else, infectious.

"I don't think quite that much, sweetie, but if you did, I'd box most of it up for next year!"

"Ewww!" Kirsty wrinkled her nose. "I don't wanna eat year-old candy!"

"I didn't say *you*'d have to eat it!" laughed Jenny.

"Maybe we'll give it to your father as punishment for letting you eat so much candy tonight!"

She sighed. Sometimes that man just did not think about things before jumping into them, and Jenny was left cleaning up the mess.

Kirsty giggled uncontrollably. "I bet he'd barf!"

"I'm sure."

"Do you think he would barf so much it'd fill up my candy bag, Mama?"

"Oh, gross, young lady! Let's not talk about such things before bed!"

Jenny reached out and lightly touched the tip of Kirsty's nose with her finger.

"Now, how am I ever going to get you to sleep in this condition? It's an impossible task!"

"What about a story, Mommy?"

Jenny put a finger to her lips and paused in thought.

"You know what? That's not a bad idea!"

She went to the self and picked up a well-worn paperback.

"No, not that one!"

Jenny's fingers glided over to a thin storybook.

"Nope! The big one!"

Jenny picked up the heavy book with the crackling cover.

"Yes!"

As she sat on her daughter's bed, Kirsty managed to bounce even higher in anticipation.

"This book is the best one, Mommy! The stories in it really come to life! Better than the other ones."

"Okay, this one it is, sweetie. Now lay your head back and let me find a good one."

Though its covers were weathered, as Jenny slowly turned the pages to find the right story, they felt glossy and new as when she herself was a kid.

"Let me see, let me see…."

One chapter page stood out. A corridor of trees with leaves of red and gold arcing over a long road.

A lone branch had fallen in the road, a slender arm with a single thin shoot reaching away from the main branch.

It resembled a numeral "6," surrounded by falling leaves. As the mother and daughter watched, a few more leaves fluttered lightly to the ground.

"This is perfect for a brisk Autumn night. We have got a toasty fire going downstairs. If you listen, you can almost hear its warm crackle…."

* * *

Glimpses of a sunset through the trees sprawled red, orange, and purple across the Autumn sky.

The wind rustled the branches and fanned the leaves like crackling flames of red and gold that arced overhead.

Jaina felt as though she walked through a warm fire on the hearth itself.

The air was fresh but brisk with the Fall sweeping through, and alive with the energy of changing seasons.

She breathed in deeply and the air smelled of pumpkin patches, spiced apples, tree sap, and the wood fires burning.

This time of year had a special resonance as Summer gave way to Winter and the changes that swept in before the leaves fell.

Nights like tonight were magic. A living dream.

She almost needed no sleep; to walk down the street on such a night was as invigorating as any night's rest.

As Halloween approached, the world came to life with creatures and half-glimpsed spirits rarely seen outside of this time.

The change was upon the world, in the rich scents that wafted through the air of baking pies, of sweet apples upon the trees, of cold drafts from distant lands, and fires upon the hearth.

Smoke drifted from the chimneys as she passed rows of houses. Orange light shone warmly in the windows against the darkening world. The faded blue scarf she kept wrapped around her neck trailed behind her in the breeze.

There was a field at the end of the street that Jaina had loved since she was a child. It was fenced off now; full of tall grass, and the derelict structures she had played with were long gone.

An old rusted tractor. Concrete chunks left from a house demolished long ago. A small hill with an old well.

She had made up so many stories about the lives that went unfolded in that place, the staging site for her adventures into distant castles and faraway lands, or lazy summer naps with her friends while the butterflies flitted slowly overhead.

In Autumn, though, with a scarf around her neck and the change of seasons thick in the air, that field would serve as the gateway to many tales. As the butterflies changed through chrysalis, as the land changed during the Autumn, so did her stories involve metamorphosis.

Jaina walked through the gap in the fence, her fingertips trailing over the cold metal links.

A shiver ran through her as she crossed the threshold, but not because of the cold metal's touch; because she had stepped across the gateway and into another world.

The grass rose up around her steps, rippling in a sudden wind. Lights like fireflies appeared above trails that formed in the grass as hidden things scurried away.

A breath of wind spiraled around her, carrying with it leaves and memory: nutmeg and spice, a steaming hot cup of cocoa in the hands, smoke from the hearth fires, a soft but warm glow as the family huddled around the fireplace and shared stories. The perfect time of year.

Everything was transforming around her. Flowers opened in the field and then fell into slumber again.

Jaina knelt down, hearing a strange sort of symphony in the growth and decline of the flowers.

A hum, like an old playground song, or the music her mother would play as they all danced between kitchen and living room, preparing a celebratory feast as fiery-colored leaves carpeted the yard. And there!

Jaina turned and she saw an aged barrel sitting there in the grass amid a cloud of fireflies and butterflies. Water sloshed in the barrel and the smell of fresh apples filled the air.

The sound of laughter and children's voices followed, and then she saw them, as though they had just sprung from the tall grass.

One of the children was her. Some of them stood on stepstools made of logs. The older ones were tall enough to stand.

They took their turns bobbing for the apples, splashing each other with cold water, giggling like mad.

Leaves of yellow and red swirled about the outside of the scene, like a shifting wall between dream and waking worlds.

Jaina smiled, seeing her older sister push her head into the water before she was ready.

Young Jaina came up sputtering, a leaf sticking in her matted hair. She had been so furious with Melanie that day!

Looking back at it, she laughed. What she would give to go back to that time when her biggest worry was her siblings tormenting her!

Turning to her right, Jaina saw another wall of leaves before her, which parted as she approached.

This time she stepped into a scene she remembered all too well: the night of her thirteenth birthday party.

Jaina's whole family had gathered in the front room with Grandma Gail; that was the last birthday she would ever spend with her grandma.

The old woman smiled at her over her glasses, saving the best present for last. Jaina remembered it well: the very scarf she wore around her neck.

Grandma had knitted it herself over weeks, in Jaina's favorite color: a cool blue, like the Springtime morning sky.

She touched the fabric with her fingertips, still as soft as ever. Some of the colors had faded over ten years, but none of its comfort or warmth.

Grandma Gail had made it especially for those cooler Autumn nights that Jaina loved to explore.

Gail looked up and met Jaina's gaze with her kindly smile. Jaina's heart leaped. A breath caught in her throat.

She stood transfixed as Grandma Gail raised a hand and waved to her.

Of all sitting in the living room, only young Jaina noticed, and she turned her head, searching for whatever her dear grandmother saw.

Young Jaina shrugged and turned back to her scarf, holding it up in the firelight. She wrapped it around her neck and beamed a smile as Gail turned back to her.

Both of their eyes lit up as they shared a special moment that would make one of Jaina's favorite memories.

The leaves shifted again and Jaina found herself walking beside a creek in a forest. Late afternoon sunlight shone through a golden-red canopy.

She remembered the area well: she had walked here often as a child, and later would bring the young man who would one day become her husband on their first tentative date.

This time she was walking behind herself, as a young Jaina balanced precariously walking along a log fallen across the creek.

Older Jaina smiled, knowing what was coming. "Watch your step!" she called, and it seemed like her younger counterpart heard something through the mists of dream and memory.

She paused, but it was too late. Her foot slipped on moss and she tumbled into the creek with a splash.

The water was bitter cold. Jaina came up spluttering and gasping for air, shocked by the frigid water. She laughed and clambered out onto the shore.

Of course, she had to go back to dry off next to a fire in the backyard, but first, she saw what had caused her to slip: a small cocoon hanging on the knot where she was about to put her foot.

She had noticed it at the last second and trying to avoid it threw off her balance.

Young Jaina found that the timing was more blessed than cursed, however: the chrysalis was beginning to hatch.

A butterfly with drooping wings slowly crawled its way out of the cocoon, taking its first tentative steps as a young adult into an unsure world.

Jaina brushed dripping wet locks of hair from her eyes as she watched, shivering but fascinated.

The butterfly's wings slowly spread as it dried in the brisk Autumn air, patterned blue upon white, trimmed with black. A first few uncertain flaps tested the air.

Both Jainas watched with a bittersweet smile; both faced similar uncertainties, her younger self rapidly growing to meet the greater challenges of the world, and her older self-having struggled with those challenges.

Even now, she had to work hard and fight to make her own place in the world.

Yet here, in the dreams of Autumn, those burdens were laid aside. For like the butterfly, as it spread its wings with vigor and took to the sky, she had undergone her own metamorphosis.

From a girl to a young woman who had made her family proud, Jaina had learned to fly on her own as well.

She watched the butterfly as it fluttered up and around her, rising into the shafts of sunlight filtering down through the leaves. A trail of sparkling dust floated behind it like a river of tiny stars.

Jaina reached up and passed her hand through it, and when she drew it back, it seemed like she held for a moment a glimpse of the entire universe shining. Growth. Transition. Metamorphosis.

As the butterfly had undergone its many challenges to become who it was meant to be, so was she undergoing her own changes.

Smiling, the older Jaina turned away. She remembered falling into the creek, but until now had forgotten what made her slip.

Now she felt that it was worth the cold and the discomfort to witness something so beautiful.

Her own thoughts rose with the wind like a fluttering leaf, whispering through the trees and into a starry evening sky.

Below her, the forest unfolded like a vast meadow of apple-red and sunshine-gold.

Ribbons wound through it in the form of the streams and creeks, helping to shape a vast tapestry.

The leaves would fall and carpet the ground in royal beauty, and the trees would stand naked in their beauty for a season.

Seeds slept in the earth's firm embrace, buds dreamed upon the branches. A blanket of frost covered all, turning to glisten dew in the morning sun.

Through it, all the land and all its dreaming creatures continued to grow and transform to find their Spring. For now, in Autumn's sweet embrace, the world slept and Jaina floated above it in peaceful memory.

In the Autumn of the year

When a brisk wind is what I hear

A cup of cocoa awaits

As the leaves, fall one by one

I am relieved that the day is done

All of my stress abates

I put my tired feet up

And reach for my favorite cup

While reaching for my favorite book

As the fire burns low

And the candles star to lose their glow

I give the room one last look

And then it is off to bed

I close my eyes and rest my weary head

Hoping that dreams find me fast

As I sleep, the night wears on

And pushes towards a misty dawn

It is the Autumn of the year, at last

The Rosebud

She is the beginning of a stunning flower

A delicate rosebud awaiting the coming hour

There in the shadows, just on the verge

She is a beautiful rose, waiting to emerge

Ever reaching for her place the sunlight

Beautiful flower wait until the time is right

Feeling so small and unnoticed, it seems

Little rosebud be patient to wait for your dreams

Your time as a rosebud pass by fast

And soon your bloom will come at last

You will open then, full of beauty and grace

And as the star of the garden take your place

,
All will stop and in wonder, they will stare

At you, the beautiful rose growing there

Feel your inner beauty, my little friend

And know that it will burst forth in the end

Fall
My favorite time of year is fall

Pumpkin spice everything, bonfires, and football

Leaves are turning orange, gold, and red

And the sun goes earlier each night to his bed

Drinking coffee and watching the frosty dawn

And watching the deer play, a mother and last year's fawn

Reading a book by a cozy fire

Remembering all the things to which I aspire

I light an apple-scented candle

And grab my teacup by its delicate handle

I settle in for a much-needed restful day

Yes, Fall is my favorite time of year all the way

Emergence

He is emerging from a cocoon

More than just a caterpillar,

He will be a butterfly soon

He struggles, and he tries

To strengthen his wings

He must work before he flies

Filled with frustration and doubt

Sure, that he will not make it

He fears he will never get out

But future before him is bright

He is wonderful and amazing,

And soon he will take flight

When his emergence is complete

We will all cheer his success

As he flies away without defeat

Summer's End

Now is the time of Summer's End

Not as much, free time to spend

Summer tourist have all gone home

And I walk the lakeshore alone

Time to say goodbye to those days so warm and lazy

Now everything is going to be fast and crazy

Time for bonfires and jumping in piles of leaves

Drinking hot cocoa, and wearing long sleeves

I anticipate the cooler, shorter days

Yet, I miss basking in the sun's rays

It happened so fast, I can hardly remember

Yesterday it seemed, was June, and now it's September

As I light Autumn's first cozy fire,

My cocoa in hand, almost ready to retire

I reflect up the season just passed

Smiling at the memories of love and laughter, always to last

Autumn's Call

Though summer's heat lingers still

I can hear Autumn's call

With anticipations, I long for its chill

I await the leaves of red and gold

And hot apple cider

To chase away the cold

I am ready for pumpkin spice

Bonfires and bobbing for apples

And a hayride would be nice

The end of summer is near

In the hot, hazy afternoon

Autumn's call is all I hear

The days grow short and the leaves are turning

The chill creeps in while bonfires are burning.

Autumn has arrived at long last

Riding in with skies, cloudy and overcast

In every window, Jack o' Lanterns are glowing

And the season's first flurries are snowing

Pumpkin pies are in the oven baking

And candy is set out, free for the taking

Hot cocoa with marshmallows fills every mug

And spiced apple cider is made by the jug

Families and friends are all gathered together

Drawn closer by the cold, rainy weather.

Autumn is by far the coziest time of year

So many stories to tell and to hear

Then snuggle under the blankets for the long night

And let all of your Autumn dreams take flight

Chapter 13 The Eagle Takes You With Him

Before we begin this journey downwards into the deepest realms of our sub-conscious, let us take a minute to physically and mentally and spiritually acclimate ourselves into being with awareness of our inner-sanctum, our internal workings. We will begin by going to a place of comfort, ideally a bed, or a very comfortable reclining chair, and we will relax our bodies to the furthest extent possible. Now, close your eyes, staying firmly on your back, with your arms relaxed at your sides and your legs rested downwards. Take one deep breath in, through your nostrils, counting slowly to four, and one deep breath out, through your nostrils again, counting slowly to four. Breathe in the breath of the spirit and breathe out the stress of the day. Now is the time to rest. Become aware of nothing but the air flowing through your nostrils, envision a steady flowing stream, smooth inhalations and exhalations, your body become weightier and more relaxed with each passing cycle of breath. Allow your thoughts to become completely still, as you focus on your core, your solar plexus, allowing your thoughts to flow outwards past your vision until they escape your being, while only holding and retaining the pure awareness of spirit, the holy serenity of the mind and body. Breathe in, one, two, three, four, then breathe out, one, two, three, four, each breath becoming slower. One... two... three... four... One... two... three... four... One... two... three... four... One... two... three... four... One... two... three... four... One... two... three... four... Continue this pattern of breath, expanding, and sink down deeper into yourself, becoming a voyeur of your own still, relaxed body, lost in time. Become lost in this experience as you journey further into the trance, and prepare for the road we are about to embark upon. Draw further and further away from your still, lying body, and into the realm of imagination, where images grow, the land of dreams that you are about to become one with. Erase your mind of all that is within it currently, and prepare the landscape for a new and fresh experience, in the farther reaches of reality. One... two... three... four... inhale... One... two... three... four... exhale... One... two... three... four... inhale... One... two... three... four... exhale... Now, with your mind, body, and spirit rested totally, entranced, and fertile, let us begin.

It seems as if all of the earth is on fire, dry, deserted land stretched out as far as the eye can see, gone up in flames. You don't look down, but you can almost feel the heat on your legs, or maybe that's just your imagination. You are clutched to your guardian, soaring through the sky, his generous, unlimited bounty of feathers molding to your frame, providing a cushion, providing a grip, providing a shelter. He soars down and you lose your stomach, he soars up and you feel a slight pull back, but know that he would never let you fall, this giant, glorious eagle that saved you from that mountain peak just before the flames engulfed it, now carrying you to some isolated safety that only he knows. You feel you are working in total tandem with this creature, you called him forth from deep inside, and he came from the outside to take you upon him. He flew down, and beckoned to you, and you perched atop him and set forth into the night, leaving behind the dangers of the world. Now you are soaring, possibly across the furthest reaches of the globe. It has been an incredibly long journey, but you are in the best company. You would be totally satisfied to never let go. Being here is like being at home, in bed, dreaming, in the most finely fluffed pillows and comforters with the smoothest silk sheets. For all you know, this could be a dream, and one that you never wake up from. The two of you converse, in silence, thoughts and feelings flowing from your skin into his feathers at the point of contact, and back to you when he is done with them, improving on them, giving you all that he has to offer, in his grand and glorious wealth of spirit. Is this creature even real? Is this some God? For all intents and purposes, it might as well be. This is heaven, this is your guardian angel, and you are flying the greatest heights ever known to man. You hug the beast, and caress your face against his feathers. A great love is brought forth in this vibration, from your cheek to his feathers and into his being and vibrating outwards back to you. He is to tell you, everything is going to be okay. You are safe here, and now, you will always be safe with me, and I will always be there to protect you. You ask the eagle where he is taking you, and he answers that he is taking you where it is that you want to go. You don't know where that is. But in the greater language that the two of you are sharing, maybe this message is as plain as day. You feel as though you are open books to each other, and awakening in each other new things just by sharing in the exposure. This creature sees you, and feels you, and knows you, like a family member, like a spirit watching you, like a guardian angel. The journey is long, eternal. You have been flying seemingly across the galaxy, and have lost track of time due to the incredible comfort and peace and serenity gained from your new companion, which has totally relaxed your mind and its perceptions. This may as well be the destination unto itself, and this journey might as well continue on for the rest of your lifetime. The grip of your body onto his back is like the completion of a puzzle, as if you have met your maker and are now having a personal conversation with God himself. You wonder where the beast came from, if he was manifested at the exact moment you needed him, if he had always been there, connected to you, or if he is just another life, alongside yours, that happened to coincide with your own at this time, just so happening to provide you with the strongest bond that you have ever felt. You ask him. His answer seems to just say that he is here, now, that being all that matters. Maybe he does not know. Maybe it just doesn't matter. This eagle is a bridge between you and eternity, for in him you feel your eternal self, as well as a connection to something greater. Even if he were to fly back to earth and put you down wherever that may be, you would still be with him, flying, here, for a long, long time. Maybe forever. This is something that will never leave you, this experience, now that it has been granted. You have been given the gift of flight, now, through this being. Wherever you are, you will always be in heaven. You brace yourself, and raise your head to peer over the great beasts shoulders. You can see the curve of the earth forming at the horizon. Whatever it was of the smoke seems to have dissipated; the flames now being long, far off behind you. Maybe the world wasn't on fire after all; maybe it was just that mountain. You can't be so sure of anything right now. Somewhere, out there, is home. You don't remember. But he knows. He knows where you belong, and he is taking you back. You realize that at this moment, whatever happened, you don't know yourself. You could be anything, or anyone, and your greatest identification at this moment is with the beast. The horizon is giving away to what looks to be an ocean, a body of water that is stretching out further than you can define. The eagle is heading straight into it. The wilderness of the land is giving way to the shore, what once was a sprawling sea of trees breaks up intermittently to become a sprawling sea of blue oblivion. The entire atmosphere changes, and the heat turn into a pleasant, breezy coolness. Is this where your home is? Is your home past this ocean? Maybe among the ocean, on a small, secluded island? Is it a home you know, or a home you are about to meet? The same to you, as you are, having forgotten all that has come before this journey. Wherever the eagle takes you. As you breach the shore, the eagle swoops down, and you become very close to the water. He wants to cool you off. He wants you to see the glimmering light of the stars, reflected off this gorgeous mirror. A billion little twinkles, a labyrinth of lights, stretched out as far as the eye can see. Then he soars back up, and, with that, you are hypnotized. You close your eyes, and you are flying through the stars themselves, alone, you are channeling this beast and he is within you, but you are alone. You are flying, and flying, and it will never stop. You feel so relaxed, your body falls, out of itself, there is only light, forever, a million light-years through space, a never-ending journey through the rivers of time, and you are asleep.

Chapter 14 Serenity

You find yourself in a vast, white room. It's so bright in this room that you can't see its walls. Maybe you've got a lot of things going on in your life. Maybe someone said something to you that wasn't nice. Maybe you keep thinking about a certain situation that really bothers you, or perhaps you still find it too important what others think about you. Right now, you can't change any of that. It's all just unnecessarily robbing you of your precious strength.

You stand there in the infinite white room and notice the turmoil within you. You take a deep breath. As you exhale, a large bubble forms around you, like an iridescent soap bubble. But it doesn't burst when you touch it – its thick and sturdy surface just keeps shimmering. This protective bubble is only permeable to air and pretty thoughts, not to all those bad things from your stressful day. This kind of protection relaxes you; nothing bad can reach you now.

The bubble rises steadily, lifting you up high into the air. From there, it takes you to all the people and situations that have been on your mind recently. You look down on them from up there. You aren't part of any of it anymore. You are in your protective bubble and keep rising and rising.

Within the bubble, you hear these words:

"Look, they're all so small."

They actually are! All the bad things of your day and everyone who was robbing you of your strength have become so small! It's almost adorable how everything bad down there seems to be busy being bad, all by itself. It feels good to watch the little baddies being upset to no avail.

They cannot harm you. It's not important what they think. They are not important.

You keep rising until you can't see them anymore.

– pause for about a minute, listening to the music –

Your protective bubble floats back into the vast and bright room. It carefully lands and then slowly fades away. You feel good and smile serenely.

Whenever you feel like it, you can return here and soar through the sky with your bubble again.

As a 'snack':

You feel your body weight as you sit comfortably on your buttocks.

As a 'snooze':

You feel your body weight as you lie comfortably on the mattress.

You hear the words echoing in your mind:

„Look, they're all so small."

You're glad about being able to let go of everything irrelevant. You can simply return here, whenever you feel like it, rising all the way up with your bubble and letting everything else become small.

Outro for the 'meditation snacks'

You just sit there, feeling the surface you're sitting on.

You gingerly move your toes.

Then your fingertips.

Slowly, you move your legs next.

Then your arms.

Perhaps you'd like to stretch a little.

[You slowly open your eyes.]

Welcome back!

– the music plays on –

Outro for the 'meditation snoozes'

You can simply stay as you are.

Feel free to make yourself comfortable with your pillow and blanket.

However you choose to lie in bed, you're now able to peacefully fall asleep.

– the music plays on –

Chapter 15 Courage

You stand in a vast, white room. It's so bright in there that you can't see its walls. You stand in the middle of the room, and a thick curtain of fog builds up in front of you. You feel like walking through it, when you notice someone standing next to you. A tiny person keeps looking over to the obscure mist anxiously. Only you know how this person looks. Suddenly, they become larger and larger until they're almost your size. But just like before, the person keeps watching the mist.

"Who are you?", you ask.

The person says: "I am Fear. Don't go through the fog; you don't know what's behind it! Maybe you won't even make it through. Maybe the fog is so dangerous that you'll never make it out again!"

Fear wants to keep you from stepping into the mist, through the unknown. You hesitate. But before Fear can become larger, you take it by the hand and step into the mist with it together.

In there, you can only see a very short distance ahead.

Fear speaks again: "You see? I told you it's not good in here. We can't see anything!"

"But that's not true", you reply. "We can see where we're going, albeit not very far."

You encounter obstacles on your path, and easily climb over them. You reach small streams and rivers, but you simply jump over or wade through them. There are dangerous areas as well, but there, Fear takes your hand.

"My second name is 'Caution'", it says, and safely ushers you around the danger.

In some areas you go downhill – sometimes even rolling! And you both laugh without a care in the world. In some parts you can even slide! It's all so much fun! Whenever it goes back uphill again, you simply put one foot in front of the other until you've reached the top. Sometimes the road is rocky and uneven, sometimes you even find stairs.

You just keep going. In the end, you reach a plateau and it starts to become brighter in the distance. The end of the fog is in sight! You take another look at Fear. It's returned to its small size, so small that you can delicately pick it up and carry it on the palm of your hand for the rest of the way.

You step out of the mist, out into the clear, fresh air, and you can see the path going on until the horizon.

"You see?", you tenderly ask tiny Fear in your hand. "We made it. We got out of the mist!"

"Yes", it says and smiles.

Suddenly you notice another person next to you, who says: "We made it. We simply kept going."

"Have you been here this entire time?", you ask. "Who are you?"

"Yes, I was there all along and helped where I could. I am Courage, and I am always by your side, no matter where you are. Whenever you feel lost, I will give you the strength to go on. Because it does always go on, you know. Sometimes Fear will be bigger, sometimes I will. But it will always go on. Always.

There's light behind every wall of fog!
Fear keeps forgetting that. But I don't."

– pause for about a minute, listening to the music –

You stand there, taking in the breathtaking landscape around you. That's the future to which you can look forward! Fear and Courage are good friends of yours. Together they help you navigate any path that you wish to take.

As a 'snack':

You feel your body weight as you sit comfortably on your buttocks.

As a 'snooze':

You feel your body weight as you lie comfortably on the mattress.

You hear these words echoing in your mind:

There's light behind every wall of fog!

You're glad to have had this beautiful experience together with Fear and Courage. Whenever you feel like it, you can return here and travel through the fog with them, overcoming obstacles and admiring the stunning view at the end.

Outro for the 'meditation snacks'

You just sit there, feeling the surface you're sitting on.

You gingerly move your toes.

Then your fingertips.

Slowly, you move your legs next.

Then your arms.

Perhaps you'd like to stretch a little.

[You slowly open your eyes.]

Welcome back!

   – the music plays on –

   Outro for the 'meditation snoozes'

You can simply stay as you are.

Feel free to make yourself comfortable with your pillow and blanket.

However you choose to lie in bed, you're now able to peacefully fall asleep.

   – the music plays on –

Chapter 16 I Love Myself

You imagine a room engulfed in a very bright, white light. It's so bright in there that you can't even see the walls! There's a child standing in the middle of the room, smiling mischievously, and looking exactly like you.

It is you! And how beautiful you are.

The child has sparkling eyes, a pretty face, and such a beautiful smile, without doing anything special. And that's perfectly fine. You approach the child, who is thrilled to see you! Both of you look each other into the eyes and smile. You hug each other very lovingly and stand there for a while in a tight embrace.

Do you know that feeling? When you hug someone you love, your entire heart feels all tingly! As if both your and the other's hearts had some sort of pull towards each other. As if both hearts created a whirlwind inside your chest. It feels good to hug that person and to be hugged by them; to be close to each other.

That's the feeling you're having right now while you embrace your younger self. To that child, you are the kindest person in the whole world, and the two of you can hug for as long as you want. You hold each other in your arms and smile.

Maybe you get emotional. Or maybe you make each other laugh. Or maybe you must cry, just because it's all so beautiful right now. You stay together like that for a while.

– pause for about a minute, listening to the music –

Then, you slowly let go, and look each other into the eyes. You tell the child: "I love you." And the child answers: "I love you, too."

They nod encouragingly until you dare to say:

"I love myself."

The child beams a wide smile at you! Then, they sit down on the floor of the white room and look away very contently. You calmly walk on, but not before exchanging another kind smile with the child.

As a 'snack':

You feel your body weight as you sit comfortably on your buttocks.

As a 'snooze':

You feel your body weight as you lie comfortably on the mattress.

You hear these words echoing in your mind:

"I love myself."

You're glad to have had this beautiful experience with yourself. You can come back and visit your inner child whenever you want.

Outro for the 'meditation snacks'

You just sit there, feeling the surface you're sitting on.

You gingerly move your toes.

Then your fingertips.

Slowly, you move your legs next.

Then your arms.

Perhaps you'd like to stretch a little.

[You slowly open your eyes.]

Welcome back!

– the music plays on –

Outro for the 'meditation snoozes'

You can simply stay as you are.

Feel free to make yourself comfortable with your pillow and blanket.

However you choose to lie in bed, you're now able to peacefully fall asleep.

– the music plays on –

Chapter 17 Dancing With Dragons

What is it we are trying to do when teaching mindfulness? In my view we are showing our students how to become aware of their own experience and the world around them, and through this relieve their dissatisfaction and unhappiness. When the Buddha was asked what he taught, he replied that he taught the end of suffering. If that was good enough for him then it is certainly good enough for me. Of course, there are other by-products of practice, such as better health and greater performance in certain fields, but for me the relief of suffering is the essence.

Dragons are fierce and scary, but also wonderful and mysterious, much like our emotional life. Our meditation is a way of learning to turn towards these dragons and dance with them, rather than trying in vain to rid ourselves of them.

Your secret practice

Most of us who practice meditation have a secret agenda or a secret practice, what one teacher called our hidden practice. Our secret practice is our deeper reason for practicing meditation, and it takes honesty to uncover it. It may not be completely secret from ourselves, but because we are rarely totally honest with ourselves it remains in the shadows. For example, we may experience feelings of shame or guilt, and of course we don't like having them. So, we take up meditation with the idea that we will somehow cure ourselves of these feelings. We may use all the right language of accepting them, letting them be, and welcoming them, but if we look with honesty, we must acknowledge that we really want to be rid of them.

People on my courses often ask me whether, if they accept these feelings, they will go away. This is exactly the reason they are still present, because this attitude leads only to more internal conflict. There is a part of me that doesn't like some other parts of me and is trying to get rid of those parts.

What we are doing here is taking profound and transformative notions of acceptance, letting be and so on, and trying to turn them into mere techniques with which to cure our problems. One side of our personality takes up arms against the other side, and of course meditation is a great weapon because it is done with the notion of being spiritual and compassionate. So the hidden war goes on.

Our secret practice is bred by a fantasy - the fantasy that meditation will cure us of anything unpleasant, or that it will make us kinder, more compassionate, wiser, more confident or whatever. Meditation can of course help us to cultivate these qualities, but not if we use it to go to war on ourselves. We cannot expect to be more compassionate when we fight against feelings we don't like. Being compassionate means learning to experience and to feel all those feelings we don't want to feel, and not just the pleasant ones.

A few years ago, my father died, my wife's eyesight seemed to be failing and my dog was ill. During that period, I woke up one particular morning feeling deeply sad. I then took myself into my meditation space and sat down. I have made honesty with myself my practice, and I had to admit that I just wanted to feel better. However, instead of playing into that game, I took my attention to the sensations of deep sadness and stayed with them. I became curious about them and just felt them. There was a ring of sorrow in my heart and chest. Tears came and went. After twenty minutes or so I felt the tension easing and the weight lifting. What had happened was that I had stopped fighting against it. All my opinions and judgments - about how bad this was, how I didn't like it, how I wished it would all go away - were absent. I felt lighter. I had allowed myself just to feel the sadness, and really that is all we need to do. This was me learning to dance with the dragon of sadness.

Our meditation practice can so easily become a means of steering away from these uncomfortable areas of our lives, when really, we need to be steering towards them. This is why honesty is so crucial in our practice. When you sit in meditation and you are honest about your intention, then the transformation has begun.

The path of mindfulness is the path of honesty with ourselves. Honesty allows us to acknowledge what is really going on in any moment. Honesty and curiosity are the two qualities that help us reveal our secret practice.

Questions are an excellent tool for unearthing our secret practice. I often use questions, and suggest my students use them too. For example, I may ask myself what is going on right now, or I may notice that I feel hurt, sad or uneasy in some way. If I am at work or busy in my daily life, I may have to decide that now is not a good time to have a look at this right now.

Once we acknowledge that we have a secret practice, we know that our students have one too, so we can help them. Of course, our secret practices are not identical, because each of us has different things we like and dislike about ourselves. One student may have unacknowledged anger; another may experience lots of shame; another may find sexuality difficult to acknowledge; another may be very uncomfortable with sadness. However, the healing of this is always to be honest and curious, and to learn how to experience these unwanted parts of ourselves.

Two pools of practice

One of my favorite metaphors is that of the two pools, from the Zen tradition. It perfectly sums up two different approaches to practice.

Imagine there are two pools, Pool A and Pool B. These pools look a little strange because they both have rubbish around the outside.

Person A goes to Pool A, jumps over the rubbish and into the pool, and has a good time. They get out and dry off. They feel refreshed for a while, a few hours. They do this day after day. No matter how many times they enter the pool, it still looks the same, with the rubbish around the outside. In fact the rubbish slowly builds up.

Person B would rather go to Pool B, but there is something different about how this person enters the pool. As they get to the side of the pool they pick up a little of the rubbish and dive in. The pool cleans up the rubbish, so when they get out with it they realize it is no longer rubbish but has transformed into something else. They may or may not feel refreshed, but they are not so concerned with how they feel immediately. The point is that there is now less rubbish around the pool, for the next time they come.

The pools represent two approaches to practice. The Pool A approach is where we just want to ignore our rubbish. We don't want to look at any difficulties, we just want the bliss. This was originally my own approach to practice. The problem with this approach to meditation is that the rubbish keeps building up. In the Pool B approach we are willing to take the rubbish into the pool with us, a little at a time, and so over time it gets cleaned up.

Although Pool A looks like Pool B, they are not the same. The first pool is the approach of concentration, often mistaken for mindfulness. Concentration is of course useful, but it is only one facet of the jewel of mindfulness. A practice based merely on concentration is one where we block out anything which troubles us. In teaching we may tell our students to just come back to the breath if something bothers them. That may help them to feel better in the short term but in the long term it will not get them very far. We need to show them how to take their rubbish into the pool for it to be cleaned up. The way to clean up the rubbish, or a better term would be to transform it, is to experience it in the body.

My question to you is: which pool of practice do you go into each day? And just as importantly: which pool of practice are you teaching your students?

The Dancing with Dragons meditation

I often use the "Two pools of practice" metaphor to introduce this meditation, which is also known as Untying Emotional Knots or Working with Difficulties. It is the central focus of Week 5 on our eight-week course. However, we cannot really help touching on this topic every week, as questions about difficult emotions are always arising.

I usually begin this meditation by asking students to be curious about their present-moment experience in the body and to see if anything needs attention: for example, a tension, a tightness or an uneasiness somewhere. This is the equivalent of picking up a little rubbish to take into the pool with you, and not ignoring it in the pursuit of some abstract blissful state of mind. Or I may ask them to begin the meditation practice with the question: what don't I want to face in myself right now? This is being honest and acknowledging that there are going to be things about myself that I don't want to face.

After asking the question, we have to be willing to be curious about where it is felt in the body and really honest about how it feels and our attitude towards that feeling. We then just sit with it and let it be. We don't do anything towards it. We don't zap it with healing lights and try to change it in any way. We leave it be and hold it in awareness. This is how change happens; it is a natural consequence of experiencing without interference and without wanting to force change to occur.

A good way of adopting this way of practicing with difficulties is to actually notice what the physical sensation feels like. Does it feel heavy or light? Does it feel hot or cold? Hard or soft? Does it have a shape? We may also notice how it feels emotionally; we may observe some sadness or anger or another uncomfortable emotion. We may notice that it is related in some way to an event in our life, such as a communication problem or a relationship.

However, we need to just hold it in awareness and not look for results. If we are looking for results then we are not present with it, and again we are into an agenda. If you are truly compassionate to a friend who is in pain, you are not looking for a result or to fix them. The same goes for being with our own pain. We just learn to feel and listen. We are not here to fix ourselves.

It can take a while, months and sometimes years, to begin to turn our attitude from one of wanting benefits to just doing the practice and letting the benefits arise.

Idiot compassion and challenging your students

Most people who walk through the door of the mindfulness room for the first time come for the wrong reason. They come in order to be fixed, to be cured, perhaps even for you to do it for them. They may come with the idea that they need to get rid of some part of themselves or to become a better person.

The Buddhist teacher Chogyam Trungpa coined the phrase "idiot compassion" to describe compassion that is unreal and unhelpful. He defines an idiot as someone who is "senseless", who does not think intelligently. "Idiot compassion" is showing deep heartfelt concern when we do not really feel it. This is often an unthinking, knee-jerk response, which might take the form of saying something like: "Oh you poor thing, how awful that must be!" Chogyam Trungpa describes this as "the compassion of the ego", because it is motivated not by genuine concern for the other person, but by a desire to be liked or to feel good about ourselves.

However, compassion in the true sense is not this wishy-washy "oh how awful that must be" attitude. Compassion in the Buddhist tradition is often depicted as being wrathful and powerful; it is not just depicted as pink lotuses. In our teaching, compassion is doing and saying what is necessary to help a student become clear about what creates their own suffering. To do this we have to use our intelligence, be honest and be willing to challenge. We have to be prepared for the student to feel a little uncomfortable, as this may be the first time somebody has challenged them in this way.

There is a difference between causing pain and causing harm. In my teaching I may occasionally have to cause some pain or at least discomfort, but my intention is not to hurt or harm the students in any way; it is to wake them up. As a consequence I may need to disagree with something one of them has said, in which case I need to be willing to say: "Wait a minute, is that true?"

At other times, I may know somebody is holding an unhelpful view but instead of speaking directly to them I may speak to the group, so it does not hurt quite so much and I don't put an individual on the spot. As teachers we have to read what is in the room. We don't always get it perfectly right, but if our intention is good we won't go far wrong.

We can only challenge, though, if we keep our own sensitivity; otherwise we could be a little brutal and that of course is out of the question. To paraphrase T. S. Eliot, people can't bear too much reality, so we challenge our students, but not too much or too soon. We want to leave them with something to ponder, something to consider about themselves and their lives.

A good challenge may not be something said; it may be just a pause, a few moments of silence. These moments can allow realizations to occur. Something may dawn on the students in those few moments of quiet.

What I have seen is that if you are willing to challenge your students, they come to trust you. They see you are not there just to be liked, but that you have their welfare at heart because you are willing to stick your neck out for them. Invariably towards the end of a course or a retreat they show their appreciation. It may be the first time that somebody has challenged them in that way and it is what they have been waiting for.

This can be one of the most difficult areas for teachers, because we don't want to be seen as mean, or we may be just not very good at disagreeing. So we can easily err on the side of caution and not really challenge at all. I think this is a real shame, as coming along to a mindfulness course is a wonderful opportunity for somebody to transform their life. Teachers are there to help this happen, not to give themselves and the students a nice time.

Working with difficult emotions and pain

Working with difficult emotions can be one of the most challenging aspects of teaching. As teachers we want to be able to work with our own before helping others. We need to be okay with feeling uncomfortable emotionally and to know how to embrace and to work through this process.

We all have unresolved emotions. A lot of our thinking is a protection against feeling these emotions. How often do we feel hurt and just keep on going over the same thing again and again, keeping busy?

I often say on retreats that it is not the emotions we experience that are so problematic, but the ones we don't. These unacknowledged emotions can become lodged in the body, weighing us down and making life feel heavy. Every one of us has to some degree what we can call unacknowledged sadness or anger, which left that way may cause depression or at least this sense of heaviness, which some people carry around with them.

When I first visited Vajraloka Retreat Centre in Wales in the 1990s, one of the teachers said something which changed my practice forever. He said that sometimes we need to go "looking for trouble". Up until that point I had seen meditation as simply a matter of following the breath. My practice until then had been to get away from myself, my troubles and my feelings, in the hope that meditation would somehow cure me.

What the teacher at Vajraloka was saying was that meditation is done with the body, not the mind. We need to be curious about the sensations in the body, because the body carries the unresolved past. He said that we can learn to read the signs in the body. I found this very interesting, so my own practice developed. From then on, when I practiced with the breath I would also have a sense of the body and what was happening in it. I would occasionally go and see what I could find, "looking for trouble", and there is often something to be found. It could be a heaviness in the chest, a contraction in the throat, a holding in the belly and more.

What we really need to do is to turn toward the hurt and feel it in the body. We need to notice where it is and observe what it feels like. We need to label our thoughts and keep returning to the sensations in the body, really experiencing the physical effects that we feel. After a time, we will find that the mind begins to calm down.

Of course, for some of us the body is a place of pain, so we don't want to be there with it. However, no matter how painful it feels, it is still our home. The key here is how we relate to the pain. I don't want to sound glib about deep pain, but whether we like it or not we are in relationship to it. Practicing mindfulness can change that relationship from one of resistance and loathing to one of acceptance and learning to be more at ease with what we find uncomfortable. That doesn't mean we don't take medication and undergo treatments to alleviate physical pain, but through meditation we can also begin to relate differently to it.

Being honest with ourselves

Read this short section, then try doing it.

Close your eyes. Ask yourself: why do I practice meditation? Don't ask your head, but drop it into your being, as it were.

Wait for a response. There will be one, even if it is a very subtle sensation somewhere in the body, or some subtle thoughts connected with the question. There may be thoughts that distract you from this deep listening. Notice these and return back to the body. People often ask how I know the difference between thoughts that are useful and those which are not. When you listen deeply you will know. There is a felt rightness about the whole experience.

Always return back to the body. Feel those sensations in it. They may be a little uncomfortable, or not.

This is our first response to the question. However, we don't just stop there.

After a minute or two ask yourself: why do I really practice meditation?

Then notice what else arises. There will be thoughts, and we can acknowledge them, as before, always returning to the body. Again, be aware of any subtle or not-so-subtle responses in the body. These can often be felt around the chest or belly area.

I don't want to say too much about this short practice as that could influence your experience of it. Just give it a try. Really this is about listening to the body and the responses within it.

CHAPTER 18

12 BROTHERS

Once upon a time there was a king and a queen who lived in peace with each other and had twelve children, but these were all boys. Now the king said to his wife, "If the thirteenth child you give birth is a girl, then the twelve boys are to die so that his wealth may be great and the kingdom falls to him alone." He also had twelve coffins made they were already filled with wood shavings, and in each lay the pillow of the dead, and had them brought into a locked room, then he gave the key to the queen and told her not to tell anyone about it. The mother, however, sat all day long and mourned, so that the smallest son, who was always with her, and whom she called Benjamin after the Bible, said to her: "Dear mother, why are you so sad?" - "Dearest Child, "she replied," I can not tell you. "But he did not leave her any peace until she left and unlocked the room and showed him the twelve shots filled with wood shavings.

Then she said, "My dearest Benjamin, these coffins have been made by your father for you and your eleven brothers, for if I give birth to a girl, then you shall all be killed and buried in it." And when she cried while she was that said, the son consoled her and said: "Do not cry, dear mother, we will help ourselves already and will go away."

But she said: "Go out into the forest with your eleven brothers, and one always sits down on the tallest tree that can be found and keep watch and look for the tower here in the castle. If I give birth to a son, I will put on a white flag, and then you may return; if I give birth to a little daughter, I will put on a red flag, and then flee away as fast as you can, and God help you.

Every night I want to get up and pray for you, in winter, that you can warm yourself by a fire, in summer, that you do not languish in the heat. " as fast as you can, and God help you.

Every night I want to get up and pray for you, in winter, that you can warm yourself by a fire, in summer, that you do not languish in the heat. " as fast as you can, and God help you. Every night I want to get up and pray for you, in winter, that you can warm yourself by a fire, in summer, that you do not languish in the heat. "

After blessing their sons, they went out into the forest. One man stopped at the other, sat on the tallest oak, and looked for the tower. When eleven days were around and the turn came to Benjamin, he saw how a flag was put on. It was not the white, but the red blood flag that proclaimed that they should all die.

As the brothers heard this, they became angry and said, "Should we suffer death for the sake of a girl! We swear we want to take revenge. Where we find a girl, let his blood flow. " Then they went deeper into the forest, and in the middle of it, where it was darkest, they found a little cursed little house, empty. Then they said, "Here we want to live and you, Benjamin, you are the youngest and weakest, you should stay home and keep household, we others want to go out and get food." Now they went into the woods and shot rabbits, wild deer, Birds and little boys, and whatever food they had, they brought to Benjamin, who had to prepare them so that they could satisfy their hunger. In the little house they lived together for ten years, and the time did not last long. The little daughter who had given birth to her mother, the queen, had now grown up, was kind-hearted and beautiful, and had a golden star on her forehead.

Once, when the laundry was big, he saw twelve men's shirts und asked his mother: "To whomdo these twelve shirts belong, but are they too small for the father?" Then she answered with a heavy heart: "Dear child, these are your twelve Brothers. "The girl said," Where are my twelve brothers? I have never heard of them. "Shereplied," God knows where they are.

They are wandering around the world. "Then she took the girl and unlocked the room for him, showing him the twelve coffins with the shavings and the dead pillow. "These coffins," she said, "were meant for your brothers, but they secretly departed before you were born, "And told him how everything had happened. Then the girl said: "Dear mother, do not cry, I want to go and look for my brothers." Now it took the twelve shirts and went away and straight into the big forest. It went on all day and in the evening it came to the cursed house. Then he came in and found a young boy who asked, "Where are you from and where do you want to go?" And was astonished that she was so beautiful, wearing royal clothes and a star on her forehead. Then she answered, "I am a princess of the king, seeking my twelve brothers, and I will go as far as the sky is blue until I find them." She also showed him the twelve shirts that belonged to them. Then Benjamin saw that it was his sister and said, "I am Benjamin, your youngest brother." And she began to cry for joy, and Benjamin also, and they kissed and caressed each other with great love.

Afterwards he said: "Dear sister, there is still a reservation, we had arranged that every girl we met would die because we had to leave our kingdom for a girl.

"She said," I would like to die if I can save my twelve brothers. "-" No. "He answered," you shall not die, sit down under this tub until the eleven brothers come, then I will already be in agreement with them. "So she did; and as night came the others came from the hunt, and the meal was ready. And as they sat at the table eating, they asked, "What's new?" Benjamin said, "Do you know nothing?" - "No," they answered. He continued: "You have been in the forest, and I have stayed at home, and yet know more than you." - "Tell us," they cried. He answered, "Do you promise me that the first girl we meet, shall not be killed? "-" Yes, "cried they all," that shall have mercy, tell us only! "Then hesaid," Our sister is here, "and opened the chest, and the king's daughter came forth, in Her royal dress with the golden star on her forehead, and was so beautiful, delicate and fine.

Everyone was happy, they fell around their necks and kissed them and loved them dearly. Now she stayed with Benjamin at home and helped him at work. The elves moved into the forest, catching scavengers,deer, birds, and little pigeons to eat, and the sister and Benjamin made sure it was cooked. She sought the wood for cooking and the herbs for the vegetables and put the pots to the fire, so that the meal was always ready when the elves came.

She also kept order in the little house, and covered the bedclothes pretty white and pure, and the brothers were always content and lived in great unity with her. At one time the two of them had made a nice meal at home, and as they were all together, they sat down, ate and drank, and were full of joy.

But it was a small garden at the cursed house, in it were twelve lily flowers, which are also called students. Now she wanted to give her brothers a treat, broke off the twelve flowers and thought of giving each one a meal. But as she had broken the flowers, at that moment the twelve brothers were transformed into twelve ravens and flew across the forest, and the house with the garden was also gone. There the poor girl was alone in the wild forest, and as it turned around, an old woman stood beside him, saying, "My child, what did you start? Why did not you leave the twelve white flowers? These were your brothers, who are now forever changed into ravens. "The girl said, crying," Is not there any way to redeem her? "-" No, "said the old woman," there is none in the whole world, as

But it is so difficult that you will not liberate them, because you have to be silent for seven years, you cannot speak and you cannot laugh, and you speak one word, and only one hour is missing at the seven years, so it's all in vain, and your brothers are killed by the one word. " Then the girl said in his heart, "I know for certain that I deliver my brethren," and went and sought a tall tree, sat on it, and spun, and did not speak, and did not laugh. Now it happened that a king was hunting in the forest, he had a big greyhound who ran to the tree where the girl was sitting on it, jumped around, screamed and barked up.

Then came the king, and beheld the beautiful princess with the golden star on his forehead, and was so delighted with her beauty, that he cried out to her if she wished to become his wife. She did not answer, but nodded her head slightly. Then he himself climbed the tree, carried it down, put it on his horse, and brought her home. Then the wedding was celebrated with great splendor and joy; but the bride did not speak and did not laugh.

When they had lived together for a few years, the mother of the king, who was a wicked woman, began to slander the young queen, and said to the king, "It is a mean mendicant girl that you have brought with you, who knows. What ungodly pranks she secretly drives. If she is dumb and can not speak, she might laugh, but he who does not laugh has a guilty conscience. "The king did not want to believe it at first, but the old woman did it for so long and accused her of so many bad things that the king was finally persuaded and sentenced to death. What ungodly pranks she secretly drives. If she is dumb and can not speak, she might laugh, but he who does not laugh has a guilty conscience. "The king did not want to believe it at first, but the old woman did it for so long and accused her of so many bad things that the king was finally persuaded and sentenced to death. What ungodly pranks she secretly drives. If she is dumb and can not speak, she might laugh, but he who does not laugh has a guilty conscience. "The king did not want to believe it at first, but the old woman did it for so long and accused her of so many bad things that the king was finally persuaded and sentenced to death. Now a big fire was lit in the yard, and it was to be burned in it. And the king stood at the top of the window, watching with crying eyes because he still loved her so much And when she was already tied to the stake and the fire licked her clothes with red tongues, the last moment of the seven years had just passed. There was a clatter in the air, and twelve ravens came and lowered themselves. And as they touched the earth, it was their twelve brothers that had redeemed them.

They tore the fire apart, extinguished the flames, released their dear sister, and kissed and caressed her. But now that she was allowed to open her mouth and speak, she told the king why she had been dumb and never laughed.

The king was happy when he heard that she was innocent, and they all lived together in unity until her death. The wicked stepmother was put on trial and put in a cask filled with boiling oil and venomous snakes, and died a wicked death.

CHAPTER 19

THE ROBOT 001

Dexter was a robotics expert. However, he wasn't good at his job. He tried to create the perfect robot, which could be used to help others, but every time he did, it wouldn't work well. They would either fall down, break on impact, or they just wouldn't do anything. Dexter was torn. He wanted to build the greatest robot ever to show off to some of his science buddies, but every time he did, he would screw up. He always wished he could do better. He wanted to create the perfect robot, and more than that, he wanted a friend.

A friend was something that Dexter was missing. Sure, he had colleagues that he would speak to, and a few he would go out for coffee with, but that wasn't the same. He wanted someone he could spend time with, he could interact with, and really understand.

One

night, as Dexter was working in the lab, he heard the sound of a thud outside the robotics department. He got up, creeping out outside, and then, he looked at the end of the hallway. There was a strange orb there. It had a brilliant blue to it, and it looked like something from another planet.

Dexter of course, was curious. He wanted to see what that was. He looked to his left, and then to his

right, and from there, crept over to where the mysterious orb was. He picked it up, holding it in his hands as he looked it over. "Interesting," he said to himself.

He hadn't seen anything like this, and really, was more curious than anything at the different state of this as well. He wondered whether or not he was just going crazy, or if he was actually finding the solution he'd been looking for. Unable to think twice, he quickly grabbed the little blue ball and brough tit back to the robot he was working on. He studied it, trying to figure out whether or not he could get it to fit in the components of the current robot he was working on. He tried a couple of times, and he looked to the different locations of this. He finally decided to throw it right in the middle, connecting two wires to it. He stepped back, expecting the robot to come to life. But there was nothing. "Just my luck," he murmured. He thought this would work. He was banking on this.

He tried another design, putting it in the middle of the chamber, connecting wires to it, and using it as a power source. When he did that, the little blue ball pulsated about three times, and he immediately looked at it with surprise. "Wait, no way," he said. He was so surprised at his luck!

This could be the big break he was banking on. The one he could use at the next convention, and the next one he could use to prove to his colleagues. He was the laughing stock, sure, but maybe this would change the game. But then, as quickly as it pulsated, it then died down once more. A feeling of disdain started to flood through Dexter.

He thought this could work, that there was a chance he could use this to build the

robot of his dreams. But all of that was for nothing. Dexter didn't think about worrying that much about this however he would head back here in the morning, to work on trying to get this set up, and to figure out where to go from there.

The next morning however, when he got to the robotics office, he noticed it was gone. "Where did it go?" he asked. He rushed around, trying to find the new robot. It was small, about the size of a cardboard box, and it couldn't go that far.

However, there was definitely some sort of problem going on, and Dexter wanted to find the robot before things got worse. He checked his office, but no sign of the robot. He checked in the main hallways, but there was nothing.

Everything seemed to be fine, minus the robot. When he heard a small scream over by the window in his boss's office, he raced over there. In front of him was the robot, on its back, struggling to get up.

"Oh no," Dexter said. He raced over and grabbed the robot, holding the little guy in his hands. The robot looked at him with big eyes, and then, it spoke. "Who are you?" "I'm Dexter. I created you. You're a robot," he said. The robot looked at him for a second, not saying a word, until finally, it managed to speak. "I see.

You're… friend, right?" Dexter beamed. "Yeah. You're my friend," he said. The robot laughed. "You are friend. Dexter is the friend. Hello," the robot said. "Hi there. I should name you. People give each other names, you know," he

explained. The robot didn't say anything. Dexter figured the robot had no idea how to approach this, or even what kind of name he could be given. That meant that Dexter was in charge of the name. "How about... Sparky," he said. "Sparky is a great name," the robot finally said. He smiled, realizing there was definitely some potential for growth here. Dexter took Sparky around, showing him around to some of the different places around the robotics department. He looked around, noticing there wasn't anyone here. He then showed them his boss's office, and then, he pointed out the garage. "This is where I'll do any tune-upon you and such," he said. "Tune-ups?" "You know, I'll make sure you're better.

I'll take care of you," Deter said. "That's because you're my friend. Right?" Dexter's eyes widened. Even he was surprised by this. he never thought that he was considered a friend by someone like this, until finally, he nodded. "Yeah. You're my friend Sparky. My great friend," he said. The robot let out a buzzing sound, and Dexter felt a happiness he hadn't experienced in a long time.

The original goal of this robot was to have someone that he could bring to the competition. He wanted to win, to show that he was strong enough to compete with the big guys. But now, upon spending time with Sparky, he began to realize something. Sparky meant something more. Dexter took Sparky around, and he showed him some of the cool places in the area. He noticed that, as he got closer to the new places that Sparky didn't know about, he was scared, but Dexter showed Sparky that there was nothing to be afraid of. Dexter took care of Sparky like he was one of his own. He was quite happier, and he didn't feel like he was held back by his lack of ability to be a robotics expert anymore.

Dexter showed Sparky a couple of cool things about life, and showed him how to be a robot, but also talk to other people. It was the first time in a long time that Dexter actually felt like he had a reason for continuing on down the path he did. He finally had a friend too, something which made Dexter happy. Dexter spent time with Sparky more and more. At first, Dexter made Sparky sleep in the lab when it was time to go home for the day, which worked somewhat, but Dexter realized when he went home, he was quite lonely. He decided one night to bring Sparky with him, to show him what the outside world was like. The first thing they did, was ride the train together. Sparky pretended to be a toy, but when he looked around, seeing all of the people on the moving car, he was quite shocked by this. "So people go on this every single day?" he said. "Yep. I do that every day," Dexter replied. Sparky looked at him and nodded. "I see. That's quite cool.

I'm mazed that you have the ability to travel like this," the robot said. Dexter showed Sparky around the area where he lived. It was a small apartment complex, with only a few places around him. Sparky almost walked off towards the park, but Dexter stopped him. "Now, let's go this way," Dexter said. Spark nodded, following Dexter inside to where he lived. It was a mess, but it was his mess. Sparky didn't seem phased by the mess in the very least. In fact, he looked almost enthralled by this, amazed that humans could live like this. "Wow, this is quite cool," the robot said. "Yeah. I mean, maybe I can program you or something to help with the cleaning," Dexter joked.

Sparky looked at Dexter, and he nodded. "I would like that sir," he said. Dexter was shocked by this robot.

Not only did he seem to care about the life that Dexter had, he actually saw it as a reason to befriend Dexter. Dexter decided to show him around the apartment, how to clean, and of course, how to cook and do other things. From that point on, Sparky started helping around the house, doing chores and other things. Dexter was shocked. He didn't even tell Sparky to do it, Sparky just…wanted to help. It was quite different from what he was used to. He always thought that he would be alone. Dating wasn't easy for Sparky, and he knew that he wouldn't ever find a girlfriend. But Sparky seemed to care about him as a friend, and that of course, was something that Dexter liked. Over time, Dexter started to become more confident.

Dexter started to work on his own social skills, to try and get better at talking to people. Sparky was always spending time with him, helping him learn how to be a good person. Over time, Dexter became more confident. He wasn't held back by his insecurities as much. He thanked Sparky for that. Sparky always was down to help him with anything and was the best friend that Dexter could ever imagine. Dexter walked around town with Sparky, showing him everything from the mall, to the local museums, to even some of the markets that were in town. Although Sparky was a robot, Dexter felt like he finally met a best friend, someone that he cared about more than he had others.

Finally, one day it happened. Dexter decided to talk to Julia, who was also a robotics expert. He showed her Dexter, and the two of them hit it off. Dexter was shocked. It was the first time he had ever gotten a date, and he was amazed by that. He thought it would never happen! But Julia did care about him. She was a sweet woman, and Dexter felt happy to finally have someone who enjoyed his

company for what it was. At first, it went from one date at the coffee shop, to another at the local pizza place. Every time Dexter wasn't confident in himself, he talked to Sparky, and he would always feel better than ever before. He felt confident, and he realized that there was some confidence there, he just wasn't always sure of himself. Then, Dexter finally got a girlfriend. It was thanks to Sparky, who seemed to care about him as a friend and as a companion. Dexter always felt like he could rely on Sparky no matter what he did. He told Sparky about his fears, and his insecurities. He also learned that Sparky seemed to understand human emotions. It was only supposed to be until the robotics competition was over.

But here he was, considering the idea of making Sparky his companion throughout the rest of his research, the official robotic companion that he needed. And he liked that idea. The night before the robotics competition, Dexter knocked on the door where Sparky rested. Sparky let out a small "come in" and Dexter walked in. "Hey Sparky. How are you doing?" he asked. "Good. What's the matter Dexter?" he asked. Dexter blushed, but then, he quickly spoke. "I was uh, thinking maybe I could talk to you about something.

Listen, I know that you and I were only supposed to work together until the robotics competition, but the thing is, I don't want to leave you. I like you far too much Sparky, and I think we could… work together," Dexter finally spat out. He felt secure, and he did feel good about this robotic companion. Sparky whirred and whizzed, and Dexter felt a bit nervous. Did Sparky want to be his friend? Was all of this for nothing? He didn't think so, but maybe it was the case. After a bit of time, Sparky finally spoke. "I see. I would like that Dexter. I like being your

friend," he said. "You're serious?" "Yes. I am your friend Dexter. Even after the competitions are over," Sparky said. Dexter leaned in, giving Sparky a long hug. It was the first time in a long time he felt really good about himself, and the truth was, he wasn't cared of the future, or what the world might bring. At first, he did worry about the competition, mostly because Dexter had no idea what would transpire from this. he wondered at times whether he was doing this for nothing. But, after talking to Sparky, he realized that he wasn't anymore. He had a friend, an unlikely companion, and the truth was, Dexter was quite happy about that. He knew that, even when things were rough, even when things seemed to; be in the toilet, Dexter had Sparky to look forward to, and someone that he could rely on. The next day, they went into the robotics competition, and the two of them had the determination to get the first prize.

It was obvious that they would do it, no matter what. When they got on stage, Dexter showed him off, and the crowd was wild. Deter won, and he was lauded for his progress and ability to create the best robot out there. He was happy, but he also felt secure with his best friend, the robot that he cared about so much, around. Sparky brought him joy in life, and he spent a lot of time with him, feeling good and happy. The two of them spent the rest of their life together. Dexter was able to keep him alive for as long as he could, and he was happy to have someone so caring in his life.

Even when things got rough, he was just happy to have a good person near him, and someone that cared about him. Every night, they would say goodnight, and Dexter was happy to have a person that cared about him more than anyone else. He didn't care about the worries he normally felt anymore. Instead, he was happy. He knew he had a friend in Sparky, and

although Sparky was an unlikely companion in some ways, he didn't regret building and creating the best robot ever.

CHAPTER 20

THE MYTHICAL LAND

Heavens existed beyond the Earth. Not above the Earth as some beings believed. Not within the Earth, as others theorized. Heavens were both beyond the Earth and around the Earth. There was a sense of separation, but it was not a physical separation in the measure of heights and distances. In fact, it was quite the opposite. The separation of Heavens from the Earth was one that came from both within and without. Rather than heights and distances, the separation was measured in depths and vibrations. This was a lesson that was difficult for a mortal to comprehend. Of course, some are able to reach the realization. Some grasped a shred of a Chaos Theory from the Core Universe.

Most were led to the conclusion by a being from Heavens. One such mortal would be Angus of the First Men. There was also Raven of the First Women. Of course, there was the Great Chief Howlite of the First Men and the Great Chiefess Lilith of the First Women. These ones, these very peculiar mortals, were led by a being they call the Sacred Flame. Over time, they had begun to grasp onto the origin of the Sacred Flame. What it truly was. The Ancestors of

Great Chief Howlite of the First Men and Great Chief Lilith of the First Women were the Wandering Tribe. The Wandering Tribe first encountered the being known as the Sacred Flame as something else entirely.

A formless, nonphysical entity they dubbed as the Voice. The First Men and First Women who left the Empire before it burned believed the Voice might be something supernatural but had no certainty. They considered the fact that it might be a being from another earth. Maybe a distant star? Or even a signal sent out across the universe. But none of them realized the truth. The descendants of the First Men and First Women, who called themselves the First Men and First Women, expanded on the theory. Somehow, these humans got closer to the truth, but further. The First Men and the First Women that led the Wandering Tribe believed the Voice was a God of some kind. A guardian, a guide, and a deliverer from horrors that lay beyond their awareness. They were right on many levels, of course. But not in the ways they thought. The god they believed the Voice was is something nonexistent in this dimension. A god to these early mortals remained something that was simply beyond their realm of comprehension. A man from the 355th century could travel to the past and project himself as a god to these folks. A true god would be something closer to the realm of the Celestial Being, the

beings of Chaos and Order, or things of the like. Those that came from the infinite. That both were and were not. The reality of the god of the Wander Tribe, this Voice, later to be named the Sacred Flame, was much more tangible. Infact, Great Chief Howlite of the First Men and Great Chieftess Lilith of the First Women stepped foot upon the very tangible realm of origin for the Sacred Flame. It was during their brief visit to the cottage of Angus of the First Men and Raven of the First Women. Angus and Raven simply referred to the place as the"Spirit Realm," but it was much more than that. It was the place that most beings referred to as "Gods" had come from in this dimension. Spirits, deities, gods and

goddesses, monsters and horrors, fairies and blessings, even the miracles the mortals might pray for. All of these things slipped from this "Spirit

Realm," which would be better described as Heaven of this universe. In this place we will call Heaven, there were many beings like the Sacred Flame. Though not all of them were nearly as powerful. This is the story of the Sacred Flame and how it found itself trapped on the plane of the Earth and banished from Heaven. The Sacred Flame had a far older and far more powerful name than "Sacred Flame," which would be unknown to humans of course.

The Great Chief Howlite of the First Men and the Great Chieftess Lilith of the First Women did learn this name however, after learning the tongue that the beings of Heaven speak. It was an old language, and that made the name and the old one. And difficult to pronounce for young tongues. The True Name of the Sacred Flame was "SAURONIMUS FLAME". For the sake of everyone's sanity, we will refer to the Sacred Flame with a nickname. Let's go with Vahl. So, Vahl's origin in Heaven was dated back to a time before most of its denizens. She was one of the first beings to come to life on that dimensional frequency.

Due to this, she was able to exist for longer, giving her more power when other beings came to life there. That is why she would be labeled as a "God" in the hierarchy of Heaven. The God was the oldest spirit known in Heaven, which even Vahl did not know. A god was one of the strongest and oldest spirits to exist Heaven.

An angel was one of the more powerful spirits, but younger than a god. From there, it went spirit, nymph, sprite, pixie, wisp, and mote. As you can imagine, theydigress in order of power and age. So yes, Vahl was considered a god of

Heaven. She was one of the oldest, wisest, and most powerful. However, she was not arrogant or cruel. In fact, her eons of existence what was once a hotheaded young spirit into a placid angel and a compassionate god.

She did have ambition. Her dream was to become the God. Since she had never met one, she believed it never existed. But there was no rush for her to get there.

For the time being, Vahl was content to coexist with the other gods and celebrate existence. There was the Golem of Crystal, Lione. He was a representation of discipline and perseverance. There was the Two-Headed Mountain Giantess Ghulu, the embodiment of patience and open-mindedness.

And finally, there was the Sage Dragon Solomon, the epitome of wisdom and foresight. Together with Vahl, these four gods stood as the four oldest of the gods in Heaven. To the younger spirits, this group was called the Four. TheFour were responsible for maintaining balance and tranquility in the realms ofHeaven and the Earth. Of them, Vahl was the oldest.

She was the illumination of compassion and guidance. Her charge was to not only guide and oversee the other three of the Four but also to watch over every other angel, spirit, nymph, sprite, pixie, wisp and mote. Given the many she had to watch over, it understandable that Vahl had many eyes. In fact, upon her entire form of silver-blue fire, which rose over one hundred feet high and wielded many limbs, Vahl watched with over one thousand eyes. Those one thousand eyes were responsible for watching over and protecting not just those spirits in Heaven, but

the ones sent down to the Earth as well. Vahl was beloved by most of the beings in the realms. Heavens sang her praises and the Earth thanked her for her vigilance in their protection. During her time as the Old God of the Four, not a soul went on persecuted. Not on the Earth and never in Heaven.

But over eons of service and dedication, one can grow blind to those closest to them. It was the Sage Dragon, Solomon, that warned her of this first. "Vahl. Often it is those closest to us that we can be the most blind to. And some may grow so close to you on purpose, so they may escape your sight. Be wary of the dangers that lurk near." "Oh, Solomon. You are kind and generous to offer me your sage advice. But I vow to you; my eyes are never blind. I watch all without yielding." Vahl shimmered in the infinite light that populated Heaven. Her flames danced as she burned with mirth. Why? Why would the oldest god of the gods not heed the words of the wisest god, the god who quite literally embodied wisdom? Solomon was Vahl's oldest friend. But Vahl was complacent. She had grown accustomed to all being wary of her ire that she did not realize some had grown foolish in several eons of compassion. Once Vahl was feared as a god. The firesshe could rain upon a spirit would send them banished the most painful ways.But even the memories of ancient beings were not so long as it should. In the end, Solomon was right. There was a plot against her. Ghulu, the Two-Headed Mountain Giantess, had raised a plot to knock Vahl down so she could wake her way up. Ghulu, without another soul knowing, had befriended the God. Little to her surprise, it was a mild and unassuming spirit. In the form of a simple

cloud, it went along through Heaven and watched all. But Ghulu, in all her evil ways, gained the trust of the God only to kill it. She planned to pin the deed on Vahl, labeling her as a power-hungry god who would do anything to be the God.

And unfortunately for Vahl, Ghulu's plan mostly worked. Ghulu did kill the God, as much as the God can be killed. In its final acts before reincarnation, the God spent its energy to cast two judgments. The first judgment was cast on Ghulu. Ghulu was branded a God Killer. This was the worst title a spirit could ever be given.

With this brand, never could a spirit enter Heaven again. But to ensure that remained so, the God shattered Ghulu. He tore her apart into a thousand monstrosities. Horrific, frog-like creatures with long and disjointed arms that wield two grotesque claws. Her back was adorned with a hardened shall and hertongue was replaced with lashing tentacles. Split into a thousand of these horrors, forever called Ghouls; the God Killer was banished to the Earth. But Ghulu was not the only one to suffer. For failing as the oldest of the gods, Watcher of Heaven and the Earth, Vahl was banished to the Earth as well.

The God reduced Vahl to a wisp, just one step above mote. He sentenced her to a penance there that would last eons. On the Earth, Vahl must be more vigilant than ever before. With no power and no eyes, she must learn how to protect the Earth and all its inhabitants. She must earn the title Watcher of the Earth before she may again earn the title Watcher of Heaven. Now that you know why Vahl was sent to the Earth, transformed into the Sacred Flame, what she has done may make more sense to you. Vahl works constantly to atone her failure.

To make up for not protecting the God and her fellow spirits, the Sacred Flame aims to become the Protector of the Earth. She will not rest until the days she does so. And without the power of her own, she has learned to world closely and through the humans who are worth it. Such as the Great Chief Howlite of the First Men and the Great Chieftess Lilith of the First Women.

She will protect the world with all her spirit. She will never rest.

CHAPTER 21

THE OLD WOMAN IN THE FOREST

As he left his front door, he looked once more into the mirror, slid his hand through his slippery hairstyle, and straightened his tie. He smiled at himself; he did this daily. He found himself a suitable pear. The sun was warm, and he flipped down his head from his head to his nose bridge. He waved at his neighbor, who was watering her plants and got into his black car. He drove away tightly, razor-sharp through the bend, the tires squealed. And the sun shone horribly on his car roof. His expensive watch shone on his wrist; this time ticked away.

The time he spent well, Silvio knew what he wanted in life and had already made good progress in his career. Of course, with elbows, he had made his way to the top. He was successful, so to speak. Investments were his thing, and he had too much money. On the way to no man's land, he drove the highway. The music loud, singing along, roof open, his slippery hairstyle remained as usual. He had no worries, never had, never experienced, seen nothing, experienced nothing, only being successful in life counted for him. He had everything with him, a good look, a smooth chat, and charisma.

The sun was too hot that day, sleepy from driving, Silvio stopped at a forest trail. Take a break, spend his day off well, relax, "relax is flex," he always said with a smile. It was quiet on the forest trail but so cool. Silvio decided to go for a walk. Nature was beautiful, and it was nice and cool. Cows in the meadow, birds that flew up when he came by, and a little further on, he saw horses walking. Silvio nibbled on a blade of grass and enjoyed. He drank something from his pocket bottle and walked farther and farther into the forest. Where he suddenly noticed a

small house, that was fun! Silvio looked at the wonderful little house, there were all glass splinters on the roof, and these sparkled in the sun, the effect was beautiful, in all kinds of colors, the glass splinters were stuck. The windows were small, but all covered with small curtains, friendly red-checked curtains. The front door was small and blue in color. Silvio knocked on the door for fun; surely, no one would live here? Silvio was very shocked when the front door cracked and squeaky opened. In front of him stood a little old woman, she was terribly wrinkled, but she smiled kindly. I like that that there will be a visit someday, she said warmly.

Come on in, and we'll have a drink. Invitingly she opened the door behind her, come beckoning him. Silvio thought it couldn't hurt, that old man, he knocked it down so, he stepped through the small front door and stood in a very narrow corridor. Come said the old woman in a creaking voice, beckoning him again. She led him to the back garden where there was a cozy little table with a red-checkered tablecloth over it, and 2 cozy chairs completed the whole. In the middle of the garden stood an apple tree full of apples, beautiful green apples.

Kirrend showed Elder Silvio his place, and she quickly brought him a jug of freshwater, including lemons and ice cubes. How nice she said again and rubbed her wrinkled hands. Silvio could think what he wanted, but what did that fresh drink taste great to him. The sun seemed unmerciful on everything, except for the garden, the coolness seemed to be itself, for it was not noticeable that the weather was so warm. There was even a slight breeze, Silvio enjoyed it. He suddenly felt very happy. The old lady offered him an apple from the tree. You can take some apples with you; if you leave again later, she offered generously.

Silvio nodded again. And slowly while the old lady was working on a crocheted, it seemed like a tablecloth, Silvio's eyes fell on. It was dark when he woke up; there was no more sun, no light, but only darkness around him. He could not move; he was stuck in something. He was lying on a bed or something. Silvio called for help, what the hell had happened? He could hardly remember it; his head was pounding. There must have been something in the drink, he thought.

The old lady came running with a burning candle, which cast shadows around them. And he saw the vague contours of a cellar around him, "What the hell is this," he exclaimed. "Twisted, let me out of here, I have to go home." The old lady smiled at him, and to his horror, she stood naked before him. Sinked wrinkled as Methusalem; there stood an old woman in front of him naked still!

What was she up to? For God's sake ... She laughed and screamed, "I caught one, haha haha, I caught one, yes," and she felt the crocheted knot wrapped around Silvio. Her smile sounded in the night. What are you up to me, old bastard,let me go! Silvio exclaimed. The old woman plunged to his sex and took him into her mouth, and to Silvio's horror, he turned out to be naked too. "Raaaghhhhhhhhhhh" !!! He exclaimed noooooooooo.... But the old lady could do something about it, toothlessly massaging his gender in a professional way.

Silvio got excited, no this could not be true? But it was true. And the old woman sat down on him, Hoopla said with a smile, and she started moving on him.

It was so rancid that it almost got exciting, Silvio couldn't remember how he had it. The summer had an effect on hormones, but this? He looked at her in astonishment, the old man how leanly she raged on him, how she moaned and threw back her head, and a toothless mouth bewildered his mind. In the meantime, hairpins fell out of her gray knot, and silvery strands of hair fell over her wrinkled shoulders; oh well, Silvio thought, she looked just like a young woman, at least in the dark. After he had come to an unimaginable height, and apparently, she too because she suddenly fell over him and was unable to wake up, maybe she was dead? Silvio thought, what did he do then? But luckily after

a while she started to move again, and got up crunchy and moaning from the bed, she cut the crochet work loose with scissors, meanwhile cutting his sex dangerously, whereupon Silvio screamed that she had to be careful!

But in the end he was free and stood up, rubbing himself over his muscles, and trying to sell the old woman a big blow, was she crazy now? But he looked into a pair of sweet old eyes, and he couldn't help but sell that old woman a blow.

She could be his grandmother, for example. No, he wouldn't do that. He understood her loneliness. He still got apples from her. And once a year in the summer, he sometimes visits the old woman in the forest and gets apples.

CHAPTER 22

JOHN DIETRICH

There once lived in Rambin, a town close to the Baltic Sea, a fair, innovative man named James Dietrich. He had a few youngsters, the entirety of a decent air, particularly the most youthful, whose name was John. John Dietrich was an attractive, brilliant kid, steady at school, and devoted at home. His incredible enthusiasm was for hearing stories, and at whatever point he met anyone who was all around put away with such, he never let him go till he had heard them all. At the point when John was around 28 years of age, he was sent to go through a mid-year with his uncle, a rancher in Rodenkirchen.

Here he needed to keep cows with different young men, and they used to drive them to munch about the Nine-slopes, where an old cowherd, one Klas Starkwolt, much of the time came to join the fellows, and afterward, they would plunk down altogether and recount stories. Thus Klas turned into John's closest companion, for he knew stories without end. He could educate all regarding the Nine-slopes, and the underground society who occupied them; how the goliaths vanished from the nation, and the tiny people or little individuals came in their stead.

These stories John gulped so excitedly that he thought of nothing else, and was for consistently discussing brilliant cups, and crowns, and glass shoes, and pockets loaded with ducats, and gold rings, and precious stone coronets, and snow-white ladies, and so forth.

Old Klas regularly utilized to shake his head at him and state, "John! John! What are you about? The spade and grass shearer will be your staff and crown, and your lady of the hour will wear a laurel of rosemary and an outfit of the striped drill." Still, John nearly ached to get into the Nine-slopes, for Klas had revealed to him that anyone who by karma or crafty ought to reach the top of one of the little individuals might go down with wellbeing, and as opposed to turning into their slave, he would be their lord. The pixie whose top he got would be his hireling and comply with every one of his directions.

Midsummer-eve, when the days are longest and the evenings most brief, was presently come. In the town of Rambin, old and youthful kept the occasion, had a wide range of plays, and recounted to a wide range of stories. John, who realized that this season was the ideal opportunity for all pixie individuals to come abroad, could now never again contain himself, yet the day after the celebration he sneaked away to the Nine-slopes, and when it developed dim laidhimself down on the highest point of the most elevated of them, which Klas had

let him know was the chief moving ground of the underground individuals.

John lay there very still from ten till twelve around evening time. Finally, it struck twelve. Promptly there was a ringing and a singing in the slopes, and afterward, a murmuring and a drawling and a master and a buzz about him, for the little individuals were currently turned out, some spinning all around in the move, and others wearing and tumbling about in the moonshine, and playing a thousand happy tricks. He felt a mystery fear creep over him at this murmuring and humming, for he could see nothing of them, as the tops they wore made them invisible; yet he lay very still, with his face in the grass and his eyes quick shut, wheezing somewhat similarly as though he was snoozing.

But at this point and afterward, he dared to open his eyes a little and peep out, however not the smallest hint of them would he be able to see, however, it was brilliant evening glow. It was not well before three of the underground individuals came hopping up to where he was lying; however, they took no notice of him, and flung their darker tops out of sight, and got them from each other.

Finally, one grabbed the top out of the hand of another and threw it away. It flew immediately and fell upon John's head. He could feel; however, he couldn't see it, and the minute he thought it, he seized it. Firing up, he swung it about for satisaction, and made its little silver chime shiver, at that point set it upon his head, and–O superb torelate!– that moment he saw the endless and happy swarm of the little individuals. The three little men came slily up to him and thought by their deftness to get back the top, however, he held his prize quick, and they saw unmistakably that nothing was to be done along these lines with him, for in size and quality John was a monster in examination of these little colleagues, who barely arrived at his knee. The proprietor of the top presently came up modestly to the discoverer and asked in as supplicating a tone as though his life relied on it, that he would give him back his top. "No," said John, "you tricky little rebel, you'll get the top no more.

That is not the kind of thing: I ought to be in a decent perplexity on the off chance that I had not something of yours; presently you have no control over me, however, should do what I please. What's more, I will go down with you, and perceive how you live beneath, and you will be my hireling.– Nay, no protesting, you realize you should. Also, I know it as well,similarly just as you do, for Klas Starkwolt told it to me frequently and regularly."

The little human-made as though he had not heard or comprehended single word of this; he started all his crying and crying over once more, and sobbed, and shouted and wailed most desolately for his little top. Be that as it may, John cut the issue off by saying to him, "Have done; you are my hireling, and I mean to travel with you." So the underground man surrendered the point, mainly as he no doubt understood there was no cure. John currently flung away his old cap, and put on the top, and set it immovably on his head, in case it should sneak off or fly away, for all his capacity lay in it. He lost no time in attempting its ideals, yet instructed his new hireling to get him nourishment and drink.

The worker fled like a breeze, and in a second was there again with jugs of wine, and bread, and rich natural products. So John ate and drank, and looked on at the games and the moving of the little individuals, and it satisfied him right well, and he observed the rules forcefully and admirably, as though he was a conceived ace. At the point when the cockerel had now crowed for the third time, and the little warblers had made their first sway in the sky, and the sunrise showed up in thin white streaks in the east, at that point there went a murmur, quiet, quiet, quiet, through the thorns, and blooms, and trees; and the slopes rang once more, and opened up, and the little men took down and vanished. John gave close consideration regarding everything and found that it was actually as he had been told.

Furthermore, see it! On the highest point of the slope where they had recently been moving, and which was presently loaded with grass and blooms, as individuals see it by day, there rose, of an unexpected, a little glass entryway.

Whosoever needed to go in ventured upon this; it opened, and he skimmed delicately in, the glass shutting again after him, and when they had all entered it evaporated, and there was not a single more distant hint of it in sight. The individuals who dropped through the glass entryway sank tenderly into a full silver tun or barrel, which held them all, and could undoubtedly have harbored a thousand such little individuals. John and his man went down likewise, alongside a few others, every one of whom shouted out and asked him not to step on them, for if his weight went ahead of them, they were dead men. He was, nonetheless, cautious, and acted in a well-disposed path towards them. A few barrels of this sort went all over after one another until all were in. They hung by long silver chains, which were drawn and guided from beneath. In his drop, John was stunned at the superb brilliance of the dividers between which the tun skimmed down. They appeared to be altogether studded with pearls and precious stones, sparkling and shimmering brilliantly, while beneath him he heard the most beautiful music tinkling a good ways off, so he didn't have a clue what he was about, and from the abundance of delight, he fell sleeping soundly.

He dozed quite a while, and when he got up, he wound up in the most lovely bed that could be, for example, he had never found in his dad's or some other house. It was likewise the prettiest little chamber on the planet, and his hireling was next to him with a fan to ward off the flies and gnats. He had scarcely opened his eyes when his little hireling presented to him a bowl and towel and held prepared for him to put on the most delightful new garments of dark-colored silk, most perfectly made; with these was a couple of new dark shoes with red strips, for example, John had never observed in Rambin or Rodenkirchen either.

There were likewise there a few sets of sparkling glass shoes, for example, are

just utilized on extraordinary events. John was, we may well assume, charmed to have such garments to wear, and he put them on blissfully

His hireling at that point flew like lightning and came back with an excellent breakfast of wine and milk, and fragile white bread and organic products, and such different things as meager young men are attached to.

He presently saw each minute, to an ever-increasing extent that Klas Starkwolt, the old cowherd, recognized what he was discussing, for the wonder and wonderfulness here outperformed anything Johnhad ever longed for. His hireling, as well, was the most dutiful one potential; a gesture or a sign was sufficient for him, for he was as astute as a honey bee, as all these little individuals are ordinarily. John's room was altogether secured with emeralds and different valuable stones, and in the roof was a jewel as large as a nine-stick bowl, that offered light to the entire chamber. In this spot, they have neither sun, nor moon, nor stars to give them light; neither do they use lights or candles of any sort; yet they live amidst valuable stones, and have the most flawless of gold and silver in wealth, from which they figure out how to get light both by day and around evening time, however, to be sure, appropriately, as there is no sun here, there is no qualification of day and night, and they figure just by weeks.

They set the most splendid and most clear valuable stones in their residences, and the ways and sections driving under the ground, and in the spots where they have their vast lobbies, and their moves and eats; and the radiance of these gems makes a kind of gleaming dusk which is unquestionably more wonderful than essential day.

At the point when John had completed his morning meal, his worker opened a little entryway in the divider, there was a

storage room with silver and gold cups and dishes and different vessels, and bins loaded up with ducats, and boxes of gems and valuables.

CHAPTER 23

THE NEXT CHAMPION

I was born in Philadelphia, or Philly, as some locals like to call it. I have always been a hyperactive kid since infancy. Mother would always gleefully describe how I never woke up grumpy and how I always greeted each new day with a smile and how I rarely ever cried, even as a baby.

How I got to walk just before I was 10-months old and how I loved throwing and kicking virtually anything around once my arms and feet could carry them. I seem to have been born with more energy than your average kid. I used to think my family is the best there is, maybe not as much as when I was a kid, but somewhere in my heart, I still feel so.

My Dad's a salesman, a hardworking and diligent one. On most days, he would leave the house very early and return late in the evening. And even when he was home, he would spend so many hours on the phone making series of deliberations that rarely resulted in money.

Well, not enough money to get me a PlayStation4 like the other kids on the block. My mother used to work as a janitor back in Philly, but after my dad's employers transferred him to Washington, DC, mum stayed unemployed for a while before working as a sales attendant in a superstore. From a young age, I always loved adventure.

Back in Philly, I loved to take really slow walks to school and sniff in the scent of the air, the air seemed to have this musty, inexplicable smell of history. One that I loved to feel as the cool morning breeze blew against my face, this is still what I miss the most about Philly. More than my friends, more than my school. Can't say I miss it more than those occasional cheesesteaks dad got us though.

I really didn't have many friends back in my elementary school days, I always loved to speed back home after school. I had no time for the characteristic slow walks that most friends, or group of friends, had after school. I'd run home to watch the older boys play basketball in the mega court that overlooked our house.

Whenever I could muster the calmness, I loved to seat on the benches outside the main court and watch them through the netted gauze as my headphones blared some hip-hop. Other times, I just stood and watched, then practice when they leave. My sister, Alissa, never seemed to understand why we were so different. Why I'd rather walk slowly in the mornings while she's in a haste and runs home in the afternoons when she's more relaxed and strolling with her few friends.

Compared to me, she'sthe rather somber and taciturn one and would rather stay indoors, solve arithmetic and read literature. On arrival to DC, life, in general, seemed to get a little better – or was it the improved environment that made it seem so? – Dad got a pay raise at work and mum got a better job two months later, anything's better than being a janitor.

Our new school was way better, there was no need for taking slow or fast walks to and from school.

We joined our peers on the school bus daily. I can still recall my first day on the bus, I hopped on feeling like the coolest kid on the block, but these DC kids seem tobe mad at me for being so cool. None of them would make space for me to the seat, each chair I found some space and attempted to seat what I heard the kids say was, "Taken!". For at least the first five rows, all I heard was "Taken!", I was beginning to think this word meant something to these DC folks and was also contemplating putting up a fight with a rather feeble-looking guy who somehow managed to look more troublesome than every other kid on the bus. And till he relocated with his parents to Wichita, I still considered him the most troublesome kid in the school. My thoughts of landing a punch on Allan's face was cut short by Derek, he beckoned on me from the back to come to share his seat.

I remember pausing for a while to observe the little-big guy, he had bright blue eyes and dirty blond hair. He did seem a little taller than most other kids, but had this aura of happiness around him. A jolly good fellow, Derek Jones. I bonded with Derek really quickly and along several lines. We both arrived DC recently, he arrived only a week before me. His dad had also been transferred from Pennsylvania State, but not from my Philly, they had lived in Pittsburgh, and many other cities, his Dad's job is quite nomadic.

Derek also had my dream PlayStation4 and his parents would let me sleepover so we stay up and play some of the coolest video games till his mum comes into his room to shut off the power and ask us to sleep. On one of those really crazy nights, we still played more games after she left, we just readjusted the curtains and turned down the volume to it's barest minimum, but what connected me and Derek the most was

our love for sports. Although we spent hours talking about the most popular sports like baseball and football, it was basketball that took most of our talk-time.

We would often sit and talk about basketball for hours on end arguing from the better basketball team between the Philadelphia 76ers and the Washington Wizards to the better player between Michael Jordan and LeBron James.

Basketball, our one true love. And we'd always talk about how dreamt of being renowned jocks in high school and how we aspired to make it to the NBA and surpass the feats achieved by Michael Jordan. At age 9, I and Derek saved up some money from the little stipends offered us by our parents to get snacks during class breaks. Just enough money to get a basketball. Oh, how we loved it! It was our biggest achievement and the most valuable asset at the time.

We'd practice bouncing and dribbling on a tiled slab in the courtyard behind Derek's family house. Derek's mum, a school teacher renowned for her strictness with kids, would always shout and warn whenever she began to hear the incessant sound of our ball thumping against the floor, "Hey you boys, do remember that's no basketball court and play carefully enough to avoid breaking the window louvres or the car windscreen", she'd say as though it were some over-rehearsed line for a school play.

We even became so conversant with the warnings that we'd recite them alongside. We thought we had it all figured out and that we could avoid breakages and similar accidents, after all, we've been doing so for almost a year of playing.

Then one day, we got so engrossed in the

game with burning passion to emulate our idols, Michael Jordan and LeBron James, we thought to try a slam dunk and smash the ball against a small round circle we had marked on the wall and we were doing just great. It was in that moment of euphoria that I picked up the ball, jumped as high as my legs could carry and struck it against the wall with more force than I ever thought I could muster.

Impressive, aye? But the ball bounced off the wall with a widely different angle and struck Mrs. Jones' car. With our hearts in our mouths, we ran towards the car to examine the degree of damage done, deep down I was hoping there was no damage done, but my hopes were shattered this time, although the side mirror was much more shattered. It was while we were still examining the damage done that I felt a firm grip behind me, right on my waist and I was being pulled backwards, I could also see Derek involuntarily moving backwards.

Apparently, Mrs. Jones had heard the sound and was standing behind us all the while till she decided to pull us in to mete out whatever punishment she deemed fit for these two moderately-insolent, excessively passionate and young basketballers. We got the scolding of our lives especially because Derek and I both claimed responsibility for the accident. I was the culprit, but he took it upon himself, the good lad he is. Derek was grounded every day after school for a whole week, even his video game console was confiscated. Tough times. The occurrence marked the end of our basketball escapades in the Jones' family compound.

We had to look elsewhere. After Derek's dark days of ostracism, wehad to sit down and re-strategize, we weren't about to contemplate shunning our dreams.

Our dreams of being highly envied high school jocks.

Our dreams of getting a sports scholarship to college and eventually making it to the NBA and surpassing the feats achieved by Michael Jordan and LeBron James. Big dreams for little guys, but we've always been so imaginative.

We still spent hours talking, just talking. More of basketball, but soon new names outside basketball started popping up in our conversations, names like Tricia and Angela, or Angie, as Derek liked to call her, but that wasn't until we turned 12 and started middle school. For now, we resorted to trying out for the school junior team and visiting the basketball court in the area to watch the older boys play. Once in a while they'd let us play with them, maybe as a result of a shortage of players or just to show us some love. The first few occasions we gotto bounce a ball with the big guys, we goofed. I was really tensed up and the urge to impress somehow made me shiver.

Although I was already growing taller than most kids my age, I felt quite infinitesimal in their midst and would often give the ball away faster than I got the ball. Derek was even playing better

than me – so I thought, though he'd often say he felt I played better – We soon experienced great improvement though and when it was time for the school junior team tryouts, it didn't take so much effort for us to get picked.

Coach Bradley Grant would often say we're the future of the game and if we keep working hard, we'll someday lead our high school senior team to national glory and land ourselves scholarships. He loved to say this whenever he met just the two of us training, he'd never say it to the hearing of the other boys.

Maybe he doesn't want to make them feel less. Or maybe he just says just about the same thing to every kid on the team to boost their morale, but that would mean we're not exceptional. I still think I and Derek are the best players in the team though, after all, we're the only three-point specialists on the team.

Our basketball skills at such a young age brought us a lot of attention. Once upon a time, all the kids said "Taken!" when I hopped on the bus, but nowadays virtually every kid wants to seat with me on the bus and in the class. My grades didn't suffer, mama always says "The best athletes also took their studies seriously", "Michael Jordan is a college graduate", she'd say. These motivated me to study and make good grades too. Although I've never been great at math and arithmetic, but Alissa who could pass as a genius would always help. At least until Tricia came into the picture.

Tricia was the best student in the class, beautiful and quite shy. Sometimes during classes, I steal glances at her. Sometimes I feel she steals glances at me too, but it's probably because I stare too much. We started spending some time together during breaks and she'd put me through some math I found complex, most times I caught myself thinking about her rather than listening to her though, but nevertheless, I preferred her tutelage to my sister.

I just loved listening to her speak. I think I began to like her in some funny kinda way as we see in movies, but in movies, such feelings usually involve teens and adults and I'm just a 12-year old junior high school kidI got to mention it to Derek, "I think I like Tricia", I said shyly hoping he won't burst into loud laughter and make me feel worse.

He assumed a straight, emotionless face

before he burst out the words "I think I like Angie", he said in a somewhat hushed tone. Apparently, he had been experiencing something similar, but felt odd about it and was too shy to talk about it, even to me.

We decided to just move on with it since we were both in it then it was probably normal. Although we still have their names popping up in our conversations every now and then.

By this time we were already in 8th grade and middle school was drawing to an end. Anticipating freshman year at the Montgomery County Public Schools. My dreams are as high as ever for my basketball and my academic career. Mama says asides being exceptional in my game, good grades can boost my chances of getting a scholarship. High school would be fun with basketball, just one thing can go wrong. Derek! Derek's dad has been transferred to Madison, Wisconsin.

When we spoke this morning, he said his mum is still contemplating quitting her job and relocating the entire family. For now, we don't know if he'll be leaving. I honestly hope he doesn't. I'll miss him, he's been there since my day one in DC and we've done literally everything together. High school would be fun and all, but much less without my buddy.

Something in me still hopes he'll stay back in DC for whatever reason. I'll turn fourteen tomorrow and I'll be starting high school next week, I just decided to take out some time to reminisce some key points of my life and dream my dreams. The future lies before me like paths of pure white snow, I'll tread carefully because every step will show. Stay tuned and watch out for the next Michael Jordan.

CHAPTER 24

THE YOUNG SALEH

Saleh woke up to the warmth around him. He tried stretching, but he winced in pain. The last thing he could remember was being knocked off by an ice golem. Dariel twirled her fingers around his black hair as she nursed him back to health. "You're up!" She said with excitement in her voice. Dariel had never seen a human and the idea of having one around totally fascinated her. She gave him soup and helped him sit up as he ate. Just then, Vulen stepped in with his catch for the day. His archery skills were second to none. He had a pout on his lips as he stared at Saleh who said hello to him almost immediately. He nodded his head as if observing his environment. Vulen was weary of humans. "Only Santa Claus is nice", he always argued. "He'll leave as soon as he is fine", Dariel said defensively without being asked. Saleh got better as the days went by.

One day, Dariel asked him, "Why were you in the mountains?" Dariel possessed so much calmness. Her beautiful hair glistened under the sun as he told her about his mission to save Faland. "Why do you stay here? I thought elves don't stay on mountains" Saleh asked innocently. "We're mountain elves" she replied sweetly.

He told her a lot of things. His problems challenges he faced and even told her about the plan with Gargoth, a huge man with a few strands of hair at the center of his head. Saleh excitedly talked about how great Gargoth was.

Dariel looked at him with sadness on her face. "How did you kill the golem?" he asked as he was filled with curiosity. Dariel waved the question off by excusing herself. Saleh got well and wanted to leave the mountain top. He gave the elves a bag of gold coins, which they refused to take. "How do I reward you?" he asked. "Just keep yourself safe," Vulen said as he shot a bird with his arrow.

"You just can't leave yet!" Dariel said to him with concern written all over her.

Her porcelain skin was so beautiful! It complemented her long, beautiful hair. "But why?" Saleh asked confusedly. "You have to learn to fight, to be safe and to protect yourself". "Dariel's Right!" Vulen added and paused "We wouldn't always be there to protect you," he said as he shrugged his shoulders and walked away. "To be a hero, there are lots of obstacles lots of monsters, but with knowledge on the right things, you'll prevail", Dariel said as she sewed.

Saleh made up his mind to stay and learn. Riches weren't enough for him, he just wanted to save Faland from all her oppressors. The goblins that ate the kids up, the one-eyed crows that invaded their farms, the heartless humans who took from the poor to enrich themselves all of them. The sun went down and Vulen asked Saleh to come with him to the woods, he taught him how to aim and shoot. Saleh was devoted and, soon, with so much practice, he was almost as good as Vulen. Gorgoth was so excited because Saleh didn't return. e wore a gladiator sandal and went around bullying everyone. He was only nice because he wanted to deceive the town's savior Saleh into going away to the mountains so he can be killed by the dangerous creatures there. Vulen and Saleh went to the woods to shoot.

At noon, Dariel came with some snacks she made for them.

For every aim that was hit on target, she divulged an important survival nugget to Saleh. "Trust no one", "Completely distinguish your enemies from your friends" "Never disclose your plans to anyone", she said to him firmly. Evening came and they retired home. "I'll teach you magic and how to cast spells," Dariel said to him with a straight face. "But I can cast spells," Saleh said in defense. "That isn't enough", Vulen said as he left the shelter. Dariel taught Saleh many magical tricks, improved his ability to cast spells. When you want to kill an enemy, look into his eyes and strike him in the heart. It rang like a bell in his ears. Time passed and Saleh had to go.

It was a sad goodbye. He had become part of them. They walked him to the end of the mountains and bade him farewell. "You can always come home," they said to him in unison. He nodded and a teardrop on his brown cheek. "Goodbye," he said and walked away occasionally looking back to see them again. The whole town was in disarray.

People ran helter-skelter. "Ghost!" some of them screamed locking their doors tightly as they saw Saleh. Gorgoth told them he was dead and his corpse was eaten by vultures. Saleh felt so sad and went to see Gorgoth who was dining with the oppressors, he claimed to also dread. His face turned green and his mouth was agape. He didn't expect Saleh to return. "Come take this man to jail," Gandhi, one of the oppressors said to the soldiers and everyone burst into laughter. At that spot, Saleh killed half of them with his bow and arrow staring deeply into their eyes. It took half of the soldiers to capture Saleh and put him behind bars.

The night passed and morning came. Saleh wasn't in the cell. He was searched for, but wasn't found. He had cast a spell on everyone there to sleep off as he magically took the keys out of the jailer's pocket. "I'll kill Gorgoth

and hang his head on the city gates" he swore. He marched to Gorgoth's home. A defenseless Gorgoth appeared before him asking why he wasn't in jail. "Because I'm here to kill you", he replied. Gorgoth laughed hard and Saleh looked at Gorgoth in his eyes and struck an arrow to his chest. Everyone around ran in fear.

He took a sword from the guards and cut Gorgoth's head off. The news spread and all the bad people fled in fear. Gorgoth's head was embalmed and placed on the city gate. The people cheered in excitement and crowned

Saleh king. Occasionally, he visited the elves and took to them a lot of

food. Saleh felt fulfilled. Faland was happy and peaceful ever after.

Conclusion

These ten tales are relaxing to hear, and perfect for those who need to catch some Z's. With each story, you have whisked away into a far-off place, a dream land where people, places, and things aren't as they seem. Where everything seems almost…surreal in a sense. Understanding that is of course, a great way to understand these stories, putting them all together so that you can hear a great tale, and one that's deep, but also relaxing as well.

With that being said, I hope these ten tales will help with sleeping. They are whimsical pieces, and they are quite fun. You've heard the many adventures that either put you in the place of the main character, or you heard some fun, interesting stories that you won't want to ever forget. These unforgettable tales will help lure anyone to sleep, no matter how good, or how bad their sleep schedule is.

Just listen to one of every night before you go to bed, and you'll go straight to dream and, whisked off by the adventures you hear through the words uttered. So, there you have it, I hope you're able to get yourself some sleep that's worthwhile, and filling.

I hope you have pleasant dreams, and I hope you're able to sleep soundly.

Good night.

www.ingramcontent.com/pod-product-compliance
Lightning Source LLC
Chambersburg PA
CBHW071624080526
44588CB00010B/1263